UNDER THEIR ROOF

MY SHOCKING TRUE STORY OF SURVIVING LIFE WITH FRED AND ROSE WEST.

Kathleen Richards

with Ann Cusack

SPHERE

SPHERE

First published in Great Britain in 2025 by Sphere

1 3 5 7 9 10 8 6 4 2

A CIP catalogue record for this book
is available from the British Library.

Hardback ISBN 978-1-4087-2430-9
Trade paperback ISBN 978-1-4087-2431-6

Typeset in Caslon by M Rules
Printed and bound in Great Britain by
Clays Ltd, Elcograf S.p.A.

Papers used by Sphere are from well-managed forests
and other responsible sources.

FSC
www.fsc.org

MIX
Paper | Supporting
responsible forestry
FSC® C104740

Sphere
An imprint of
Little, Brown Book Group
Carmelite House
50 Victoria Embankment
London EC4Y 0DZ

The authorised representative
in the EEA is
Hachette Ireland
8 Castlecourt Centre
Dublin 15, D15 XTP3, Ireland
(email: info@hbgi.ie)

An Hachette UK Company
www.hachette.co.uk

www.littlebrown.co.uk

To my daughter Hannah – without her I wouldn't
be here to tell my story.
She has helped me through some very dark times.
Thank you Hannah xx

UNDER THEIR ROOF

PROLOGUE

My stomach froths with uncertainty as I reach for the doorknocker. Heavy footsteps on the other side are drowned out by the thumping of my heart.

'What if these people are even worse than Mum and Dad?' I whisper to my sister, Deirdre.

'Is that even possible?' she replies, rolling her eyes and, despite the tension, I giggle.

The door swings open and, to my surprise, the man standing before us looks unexpectedly benign and ordinary. He has an air of respectability too, in a smart grey jacket, a shirt and dark trousers. *So this is the famous Fred West*, I think to myself.

'Have you any rooms, please?' I ask timidly. 'Me, my sister and her baby.'

'Ah yes, we do.' He smiles, and shows us inside with a welcoming flourish of his hand.

Deirdre parks the pram in the hallway and we follow him into a cramped and messy living room. The TV is blaring above a hum of steady chatter. There are so many children – squashed onto the sofa, lolling on the floor, two younger ones squabbling over a melting chocolate biscuit.

This place looks just like home, I tell myself.

As I take a deep breath in, I feel my nerves draining away. There is such comfort in this chaos. I pick up a faint whiff of lamb stew; it even smells like home. It's going to be all right here, after all. I can just sense it. We stand in the living-room doorway, wide-eyed and watchful, as the man, about the same age as my dad, clears his throat above the noise of the television.

'I'm Fred West.' He grins, and we smile back politely. 'This is my wife, Rosemary,' he adds, pointing to a grim-faced woman sitting rigid in her armchair. 'And this' – he turns to a teenage girl – 'is my lover, Shirley.'

It is clearly a joke, though nobody is laughing. Fred is middle-aged and the girl looks around seventeen, the same age as me. Perched on the arm of the sofa, she is small and slight and has a small pregnancy bump. I search her face for signs of denial or disgust, but she simply nods shyly in my direction.

'Come on, I'll show you to your room,' says Fred.

As he ambles past me, his sour smell of baked-in sweat is an assault on my senses. Deirdre and I scurry upstairs after him and we're directed to the end bedroom, which overlooks the back garden. There is a double bed for me and Deirdre, and Fred goes off to find a cot for the baby. As I throw my bag onto the bed, I spot a row of neatly drilled holes along the bedroom wall.

'Look,' I whisper. 'Are they spyholes?'

Fred returns with the cot; but the moment he's gone we examine the holes again.

'They look deliberate,' Deirdre agrees, peering more closely.

'Maybe Fred is a dirty old man. That might explain why he has a wife and a lover both in the same room.'

'Oh, he was joking,' I tell her. 'He's old enough to be that girl's dad. No way he was being serious. I'm sure there's a simple explanation for that.'

Even so, the peepholes make me uncomfortable. In the gloom of the early evening, they seem to stare back at me, a row of six eyes, blank and black. I can't turn my back without fearing I'm being watched. There are sheets of newspaper covering the floorboards where the faded carpet doesn't quite meet the wall, and I rip off strips and scrunch them up to block the holes one by one.

'There,' I say. 'He won't see a thing now.'

It's been a long day and, after sharing a packet of digestive biscuits, Deirdre and I have an early night. Undressing, I rinse my favourite blue T-shirt under the tap and drape it over a wooden chair, hoping it might be dry for tomorrow. Lying under a coarse green bedspread, I tell myself how lucky we are to have found this place; cheap, clean and friendly. Yet a gnawing feeling of unease, like an unwelcome guest, floats around the shores of my consciousness. As I drift off to sleep, the worry sits like a stone inside my stomach.

And in the morning, as I open my eyes, I see the six balls of newspaper, pushed back out of the holes, lying on the floor in defeat. I don't know what scares me more, the peeping Tom himself or the fact that he is so blatantly shameless. Though the early streaks of sunshine warm the room, a violent shiver runs through me. The six black holes continue to stare, dark and hollow, with their secrets hidden safely inside.

1

Dublin, November 1966

I had barely opened my eyes when the scramble began. The dash from our ancient double bed to the dusty airing cupboard on the landing was like an Olympic sport. And the reward – a clean pair of socks and undies – was far more precious than any gold medal. Under the covers, there was a tangle of arms and legs as I tried to establish which limbs were my own. Our home was so overcrowded, our lives so intertwined, that I could almost forget where one sibling ended and another began. The lines between us, and with them our very identities, were blurred and uncertain.

'Maggie, you're lying on my foot,' I complained. 'It's completely numb.'

Sharing a bed with my eight siblings was at once cramped and cosy. If one wet the bed, we were all soaked to the skin. And with clean clothes in short supply, it was a case of first come, first served.

'Save some for me!' I yelled, twisting myself out of the sodden sheets and tripping over onto the threadbare rug. 'Remember, I didn't get any yesterday?'

But this was survival of the fittest, and on a chilly November Dublin morning in 1966, it was everyone for themselves. By the time I had limped out of the bedroom, the airing cupboard was empty.

'Last again!' teased my brother, Danny, his eyes dancing with mischief. 'You need to get up earlier, Kathy.'

Like the low winter sun, my already weary heart sank a little further. My socks and knickers stank of stale urine. Yet I had no choice but to wear them again for school. And in the kitchen, the battle continued: nine children, pecking like nosy magpies at three stale slices of bread. My shoulders sagged with defeat as I slipped out of the front door, bone-cold and hungry, with a biting wind whipping round my bare legs and the stench of home clinging to my skin as though I were wrapped in it. Choking back tears, I felt an arm around me and a friendly squeeze on my shoulder.

'You all right, Kathy?' asked my older sister, Deirdre. 'Listen, I sneaked a pair of undies off the fireguard for you. They're a bit damp but at least they're clean. They're in my bag. You can put them on when we get to school.'

And just like that, the sun came streaming through the clouds. Basking in the glow of my sister's love, I turned to hug her. That small slice of kindness, that show of solidarity, meant the world to me. The cold and the hunger mattered so much less when we had each other. For whatever came our way, we faced it together.

The fourth eldest of nine, I was born in January 1960, and the only one of the brood to be delivered at home. I had been a small baby and, right through my childhood, I was shorter and lighter than average. My fair hair, shoulder length with a fringe, was washed only monthly, and occasionally trimmed by my mother. Bathing and hair washing involved heating pans on the stove and carrying them upstairs to the bathroom. It was such a faff and often one of my older siblings would jump in to steal my bathwater while I was stuck in a bottleneck of children on the landing with my pan. I never cleaned my teeth – I didn't even own a toothbrush and had never seen a dentist. But what upsets me most, looking at rare childhood photos, are my dirty nails. Most of the time they were black with mud. Absolutely filthy. I was so ashamed that I used to curl my fingers up to hide them. For even as a small girl, hygiene was important to me, and I loved to clean. I was forever scrubbing the hearth, bleaching the sink and brushing the floors.

'You're a homemaker,' my mother told me. 'And that's because you were born right here at home.'

I loved the idea that I had some kind of special connection with our home. Each afternoon, when school was done, I'd set to work tidying and polishing. My older siblings nicknamed me 'Kathy the Cleaner', and if there was supposed to be a sting in there, then it was lost on me. I didn't mind one bit, and I cleaned in the way that other little girls did jigsaws or dressed their dollies. Yet my talents only went so far, and I could do nothing about the missing tiles in the bathroom or the cracks in the big white kitchen sink or the cold draught which crept in under the doors. We had only two bedrooms, one for our parents and one for the kids. Our corporation flat on the middle floor of a three-storey block in Dolphin's Barn, Dublin, was far too small. In addition to the adults and children, we had an Alsatian dog, named Duke, who lived in the coal bunker in the hallway and survived on potato skins donated by the neighbours. He was gentle and loving and I adored him. He was more affectionate than either of my parents. Our kitchen was old-fashioned and poky, with a small Formica-topped table and a single dining chair, shoved into the corner. There was no room to eat, no space for us to sit and dine as a family. That tired old dining table with its lonely chair was a perfect metaphor for our parents' approach to food. Mum made stews, but they rarely lasted. She'd buy a batch loaf, but it was never enough. Dad served up a stringy sort of meal sometimes, which he claimed was rice, but it was virtually inedible. Most of the time, the cupboards were almost empty. And any meals were eaten on the living-room sofa, in front of the black and white telly. There was no remote control and so I always had to be ready to change the channel whenever my dad barked out an instruction. He liked to sit and smoke in the evenings, and the smoke rings from his cigarettes would drift, wraith-like, through the gloom of the darkened room. Fascinated, I would stick out an index finger to pierce the middle of the ring, invariably disappointed as it dissolved before my eyes, as illusory and unreliable as a family dinner.

But though my siblings and I were skinny and underfed, our parents, oddly, were not. Dad was tall and good-looking, with Brylcreemed hair that glistened like a slug under the light. He had a terrible temper too, preceded always by his fingers drumming loudly, like a far-off storm rolling in from the hills. I lived in fear of that tapping noise. Any laughing in the big bed was instantly silenced with a whack of his belt. Even loud breathing, while he was watching telly, was forbidden. When I was very young, he collected scrap and sold firewood on his horse and cart. He let me ride up front with him sometimes and I loved the wind blowing in my face when our brown and white horse, Jacko, broke into a fast trot. It felt like we were flying through those streets, hanging on for dear life. Dad had his own yard, around a fifteen-minute walk from the flat, and at weekends I'd walk up the canal path to see Jacko. I loved brushing him and telling him all my troubles.

'Had no breakfast today, Jacko,' I'd say, as my stomach rumbled loudly. 'I'll be after some of your hay soon.'

He and Duke were such good listeners. Later, Dad bought a car, a light blue Triumph Herald with brown seats, and Jacko was made redundant. I tried not to think too much about what became of him. Dad could not read or write and, after I started school, it was my job to sit in the passenger seat and read out the road signs and directions while he drove. My own reading skills were patchy and the task was nerve-racking, knowing that if I gave him the wrong instruction, his big hand would fly off the wheel to slap me in the face. Dad had a brief spell as an ice-cream man and, again, I was enlisted to help with directions and also to sell ice cream, as 'Under the Willow Tree' tinkled out from our tinny speaker. It felt like the worst torture, serving cones slathered in chocolate sauce and topped with flakes, while my own stomach was rumbling and groaning in protest. Once a week, Dad parked up around the corner from the labour exchange and left me in charge of sales while he nipped inside to claim unemployment benefit. Aged seven, I paid no attention to his dishonesty. In fact I was glad of it, for I was engaged in subterfuge of my own, stuffing myself with as many chocolate flakes as my mouth could hold before he returned.

'All in order?' he'd ask, as he climbed back into the driver's seat, and I could only nod, as my cheeks bulged with stolen goodies.

Dad was not a big drinker because he suffered with particularly bad hangovers. But after an occasional night on the Guinness, he would bellow demands, like an angry ogre, from his bedroom.

'Kathleen! Bring me a cold facecloth and a basin! And' – here his voice reached a roar – 'bring it now!'

Like a skittery lamb, all arms and legs, I'd tumble down the stairs, racing around the kitchen to find a basin, knowing that if I was not quick enough, I'd get a good hiding. Dad's headache was somehow never so serious that he couldn't miraculously dive out of bed to give me a crack of his belt. And I had no idea how a damp facecloth might cure a hangover, but I knew better than to ask.

My mother had dark, curly hair and was a little younger than Dad. She was twenty-six when I was born. She was small, around 5 feet tall, but stoutly built – even a little plump. She wore a large apron with pockets, roomy enough to hide her pregnancies. Us older ones had no idea she was having a baby until it arrived home, without ceremony, from the hospital.

Once, when I dared ask her why I was skinny and she was not, she told me, 'You can't fatten a thoroughbred.'

Her reply did nothing to help my hunger pains. Though she didn't have Dad's temper, Mam always seemed cold and unaffectionate. There were no hugs, no compliments, and she smiled at me as rarely as she cooked for me. Mam once confided that, as a child herself, she had been sent to reform school for stealing clothes off washing lines to keep herself warm.

'When I wet the bed, the nuns wrapped me in the sheet and paraded me in the big hall for everyone to laugh at,' she told me.

My heart stung with sadness for her and for all she had suffered. And though my parents were distant, cruel even, I try not to judge them for their failings. As an adult, I now realise they simply were not equipped to cope with parenthood. They had been born into poverty and hardship and the cycle continued through me and my siblings. As a child, though, that was difficult to take, and I especially longed for some affection from my mother. I worked hard to try to win her love and approval. Mam liked to go to the local pub for a vodka and lemonade, probably more as an escape than a social event. On those evenings, I took charge, getting the little ones ready for bed. On cold evenings, I ran basins of warm water, so they could soothe their freezing fingers and toes. Mam did not always have time to do the laundry and so I helped out, swirling the smelly sheets and nighties in a large dolly tub before feeding them into a mangle. Like our neighbours, we had a washing line in a central courtyard. And, of course, I cleaned. Cleaning was my escape, a catharsis as well as a burgeoning career. Yet no matter how our home shone and sparkled, Mam never seemed to notice. I often remembered her words, that I had been born at home, and that was why I loved to keep it so clean. I had a special connection with my home and I only wished I could have shared it with my parents too.

2

Waking in the usual knot of arms and legs, I was preoccupied by a dream so wonderful that I was reluctant to let it go.

'I dreamed I had a big bag of sweets,' I told Deirdre longingly. 'I can still taste them now, all different colours and flavours. I had strawberry, blackcurrant, lemon and lime. Oh Dee, they were lovely.'

But downstairs, with no breakfast waiting, I soon snapped back into reality. I left for school with my empty stomach complaining loudly. I was dizzy with hunger. Trudging along, staring at the pavement, I spotted a ball of chewing gum, glued to the ground. There were small ridges on the surface, tiny dividing lines, where a shoe had squashed it flat. It was grimy and grey. It was old and dirty. Yet all I saw was a sweet. Or the nearest I would ever get to a sweet. Bending down, I pulled at the gum until it lifted, in one solid lump, from the pavement. There were cars driving past, people hurrying by, yet I paid them no attention. I didn't bother hiding what I was doing. Thinking only of sweets, I popped the gum into my mouth and began to chew. It was hard going, like chewing a frozen stone, but I persisted. And the faint yet tantalising promise of minty flavour, hidden under the shoeprint and the filth, was enough to make me chew harder.

'I found a sweet,' I told my pals, when I reached the playground, and I made the most of their envious stares as I chewed. It was rare that I had something everyone else wanted.

That weekend, I was out playing hopscotch with Deirdre and a gang of local kids when I had an urge for another shot of sugar. Having tasted it once, I had opened a Pandora's box of temptation, and it was all I thought about.

'Let's go looking for pennies,' I suggested to my sister. 'On the posh road.'

We knew from experience we were far more likely to come across lost pennies on the streets where the big, haughty houses stood back from the main road, shielded by trees and gates.

'OK,' she agreed.

Off we went, with hope in our hearts, but it didn't last long. Up and down the grand avenues we trailed, staring doggedly at the floor but finding nothing.

'I'm starving,' I complained. 'I'd do anything for a sweet. Just one sweet.'

Deirdre stopped and nodded towards a gateway, where a dustbin was waiting to be emptied.

'Let's have a look in there,' she said. 'You never know.'

Like excited fieldmice we scurried over, lifting the heavy tin lid and rooting unashamedly through somebody else's rubbish.

'Nothing,' I sighed, holding my nose as I picked up a rotting chicken carcass. 'I'm definitely not eating that.'

But it had sparked our enthusiasm, and we went from house to house, from bin to bin, lifting lids and sifting through one pile of rubbish after another. The afternoon light was beginning to fade when, peering into yet another bin, I let out a yelp of excitement.

'Deirdre!' I yelled. 'Come here! I've found a bag of cakes!'

Sure enough, inside a paper bag were half a dozen of what I would later recognise as doughnuts. To me, they were an exotic sort of cake. I'd never seen anything quite so lovely in my whole life. Savouring each sugary mouthful, our hearts brimming over with contentment, we walked slowly home to share our treasure with our siblings and Duke. It did not occur to my seven-year-old self to feel in any way embarrassed or ashamed at scraping chewing gum off pavements or finding stale food in bins. If anything, I was rather pleased with myself. Neither did I dwell on my dwindling standards of hygiene. But when I arrived home, I rolled up my sleeves and set about scrubbing the surfaces and floors, scrubbing away the footprint off the chewing gum, scrubbing away the grease and mould from the dustbins. I scrubbed and scrubbed until my fingers were red raw. Even then, I was vaguely aware that no amount of cleaning would ever be enough.

My days were marked out by stark disparity: my own hunger in contrast to the full bellies of the adults around me. The filth of the pavement chewing gum set against my obsession with cleanliness at home. The love and affection I longed for and the lukewarm response from my parents. And, somewhere in the middle, lost in the fog and confusion, was me.

Our expeditions around the posh bins continued, but we never again found anything so glorious as the bag of doughnuts.

Occasionally, one of us would find a penny or a halfpenny, enough for a chew from Sadie's, the shop further along our street. In addition to an array of sweets, there were packets of Kimberley and Mikado biscuits lined up on the counter.

'You could run in and pinch those biscuits,' said one of my siblings as we walked past Sadie's one Saturday afternoon. 'Nobody would catch you, Kathy. You're too fast.'

At first, the idea seemed preposterous. First and foremost, it was plain wrong. We had been raised as Roman Catholics and I had visions of being thrown into the burning fires of hell, with one solitary chocolate biscuit melting in my hand as I screamed for mercy.

'It's not really wrong, though, is it?' persuaded my brother. 'We're hungry. We've no money. This is the kind of thing Jesus would approve of. Remember the water and the wine miracle?'

Perhaps I believed the propaganda or, more likely, I wanted to believe it. I was so hungry, I didn't really care whether my food came from a bin or whether it was stolen. Taking a deep breath, I ran into the shop, which was long and rather dimly lit, with sawdust on the floor. Reaching the counter, I grabbed the first packet of biscuits I saw and sprinted back out. Sadie had been busy arranging her shelves, with her back to me, and hadn't even known I was there. It was all so easy. Almost disappointingly so. The cheer from my siblings and the rush of adrenaline left me breathless. And, of course, the real treat was the biscuits themselves. We had enough for two each, and every bite was heavenly. At 6 p.m. each night, the Angelus bell rang out around the city and, like many thousands of others, we hurried inside and fell to our knees in front of the television. It was left to the eldest sibling present to start the prayer:

'Hail Mary, full of grace . . .'

With my head bowed and my eyes closed, I usually prayed fervently for food. But today, with biscuit crumbs around my mouth betraying my sin, I was awash with shame.

'I'm sorry,' I whispered. 'We were hungry. But the biscuits were lovely. They really were.'

As with most children, my regret, overwhelming on that first day, was quickly diluted and forgotten. And the next time we walked past Sadie's and spotted an empty counter, my stomach grumbled as if to remind me.

'I'll go,' I said confidently. 'I'll get those same biscuits as before.'

Again, I came out with the prize, no problem. Again, when the Angelus bell tolled, I was gripped with a crippling but ephemeral guilt. By confessing my sins during my prayers, I felt as though I was wiping the slate clean, ready to go again. We made our confession, communion and confirmation through school, and I attended confession weekly. In the gloom of the confessional box, I repeated the same script each time, without variation: 'Bless me, Father, for I have thought a bad thought, and I have said a bad word.'

It did not occur to me to share more egregious issues and certainly not my budding career as a shoplifter. I wasn't sure the priest could handle that level of villainy. Besides, I could never have confessed an actual, real-life sin. That just wasn't how it worked. Neither did I dwell on the fact that I was telling lies by omission, even in confession! It was, nevertheless, a comfort to have the protective arm of the Catholic faith around me, absolving me every time I stole a packet of biscuits.

But as the weeks passed my confidence inevitably gave way to sloppiness. I no longer worried about getting caught until, one day, with my hands on the biscuits, an angry voice shouted, 'Hey! Put those back!'

Frozen for a split second, I dropped the biscuits onto the floor and ran for my life. I could not have been more terrified if the whole of the Irish Garda was after me.

'Quick!' I screamed at my waiting siblings. 'Run! Run!'

I vowed that that was the end of my shoplifting spree at Sadie's. That night, at the Angelus, I prayed not for forgiveness but for food. But it seemed the latter was even harder to come by.

With a shortage of basic necessities at home, it is perhaps not surprising that we did not receive gifts for our birthdays or Christmas. If ever I asked my mother if I could have a present for my birthday, her reply was always the same: 'You can have a kick up the arse.'

But worse than the lack of gifts, inexplicably, there was no form of celebration at all, not even at Christmas. In my mind, Christmas was for posh people only. Christmas trees and gifts and presents were for the families in the big houses and not for the likes of me. I grew up with the certain knowledge that Santa did not exist. On Christmas Day, we would sometimes have roast chicken with potatoes. But aside from attending Mass, there was no other celebration. One Christmas, the best ever, I received a gift wrapped in old newspaper and inside was a doll with one leg and no clothes on. It did not matter that she was grubby and naked, nor that her hair had been snipped short and spiky so that she looked as though she'd just had an electric shock. It did not bother me in the slightest that she had clearly come from the local dump, where Dad was often found foraging for bargains. I was thrilled with her.

'Hello, dolly,' I beamed. 'I'm going to call you Polly.'

I spent the day bathing her and wrapped her in a towel until I found an old T-shirt with holes in. I soon cut it down to size. Polly came everywhere with me, tucked under my arm as I played outside. Or I might prop her up on the hearth as I swept and dusted. And despite the overcrowded bed, I made sure Polly got a spot, right next to me. We were inseparable.

'You'll be just fine without your leg,' I promised her. 'When I'm all grown up, I'll buy you a new one. I promise.'

The following Christmas, I hoped perhaps I might get a leg for Polly. But she was the first and last gift I ever got. Our birthdays, too, passed without so much as a cake or a candle. The only 'Happy Birthday' I ever heard was from my teacher, when she read out the register.

At school, I had the nickname 'Smelly' because of my urine-soaked clothes. I wore a grey uniform from the charity shop, but my mother scoffed when I told her I needed a PE kit too. Instead, I was made to do PE in my vest and knickers, a punishment so humiliating that I cried and cried until I passed out with a seizure. When I came round, I was lying on the floor of the changing room with a teacher peering down at me.

'Did you have breakfast today?' she asked, and even though there was no such thing as breakfast in our house, I nodded mutely. The teacher sat me on a little chair outside the church next door and gave me a currant bun and a glass of milk.

'I think you'll feel better once you've had the bun and some fresh air,' she said, smiling. 'But you need to ask your Mammy to take you to the doctor.'

But again, Mam dismissed the suggestion out of hand.

'You were in hospital with seizures when you were small,' she said. 'You've grown out of them now. You're fine.'

Children in those days did not need presents or PE kits or trips to the doctor. Children in those days did not need care and affection and love. Looking back, as a mother myself, this seems dreadfully sad but at the time it didn't really bother me. There were many families in exactly the same situation as us. And it wasn't as if we didn't have fun – we played out for hours, with a skipping rope or a ball or a stubby chalk for hopscotch. We had a game called edging, throwing a tennis ball against the kerb. Though we never had holidays as such, Dad occasionally crammed us all into the car, piled on top of each other as though we were trying to break a record. He drove us to the seaside at Sandymount or Portmarnock, and all the way there, we had to sing, 'Daddy's taking us to the sea today.'

When we arrived, he barked, 'Go on, enjoy yourselves!' as we spilled out onto the sand.

At first, it seemed like great fun. But we didn't have buckets and spades. Mam would never pack a picnic and we were not allowed to buy a drink or an ice cream. And so, as the hours passed, the little ones would start to grumble and the older ones would eye Dad uneasily, checking his fingers for the telltale taps, knowing his temper might be about to blow. Looking back, I am not sure why we made those seaside trips. They were not enjoyable, and it seems to me now they were more for show than anything else. Dad wanted our neighbours and relatives to know we had been to the seaside and whether or not we enjoyed his forced fun was immaterial. Coming back from one trip to the beach, the heavens opened and it began to rain hard. Halfway home, the windscreen wipers on the Triumph shuddered and then gave up completely. Dad was furious, as though it was our fault, and passed a rag over to the back seat.

'Deirdre, you dry the window while I drive!' he instructed.

Even for him, it was a ludicrous idea. Poor Deirdre was virtually lying across Dad's right shoulder, leaning perilously out of the driver's window, as she tried – and failed – to keep the windscreen clear. Dad showed no signs of slowing down or taking extra care as we hurtled along, through the rain, with virtually no visibility. He might as well have been driving blindfold.

Eventually, Deirdre whimpered, 'My arm is so tired.'

And with that, my heart sank for I knew exactly what was coming next.

'Kathleen!' Dad shouted. 'You take over!'

It felt like a circus act, balancing partly on my dad, partly on the window frame, as my arm flapped about with the rag like a demented seagull. Deirdre hung onto my feet as I dangled half in, half out of the window. I couldn't work out whether it was more likely Dad would crash through poor visibility or I would fall from the moving car. In any event, it was such a relief to get home alive.

3

The biggest pleasure of my childhood, without doubt, were the visits from my Aunt Frances, who was married to Mam's brother. She had no children herself but despite – or perhaps because of – this, she adored her nieces and nephews. She visited us most evenings, often when my mother was in the pub. Aunty Frances had long, dark tresses and as soon as she walked through the door, I'd sit her down so I could brush her hair. I felt like I was brushing the hair of a princess. Aunty Frances always wanted to hear about my day; she liked looking at my schoolbooks and appraising my housework. When I got older, she taught me to cook. She was a fantastic chef and made everything from scratch – Irish stew, roast dinner, curry and bolognese. She taught me how to knit, too, and under her instruction I managed to produce a jumper for one of my little brothers.

'It's absolutely brilliant, Kathy!' she exclaimed, as I held it up to show her. 'You are such a clever girl.'

I blushed and hung my head, unused to praise and unsure how to respond. 'I'm going to knit a coat for Polly next,' I told her. 'If I can find any spare wool.'

But the best thing by far about Aunty Frances were her hugs. At the start and end of each visit, she would wrap her arms around me and pull me in close, the scent of shampoo mingled in with the fresh smell of home baking. It was like being tucked up under a soft warm blanket. And as her arms encircled me, I felt my worries lifting and dissipating, as though she were taking them all on for herself.

'I love you, Aunty Frances,' I whispered.

And I knew she loved me back. Those hugs were something special. I've never had a hug like it since, and I don't believe I ever will again.

Sinking onto the bench, my cheeks flushed and my heart still racing, I opened my hand to inspect my apple.

'It's so nice,' Deirdre said, biting into hers. 'Try it.'

I was eight and a half years old, and it was the summer holidays of 1968. Without the daily currant bun and glass of milk at school, we were hungrier than ever. And so passing the local greengrocer's, with boxes of fruit piled outside, Deirdre and I had helped ourselves to a shiny red apple each. We were not so brazen that we could pull it off by simply strolling past. Even though nobody had seen us, we still ran as fast and far as we could, panting for breath with a combination of excitement and exercise.

'You're right,' I nodded as I crunched into mine. 'They're tasty.'

Legs outstretched, faces towards the sun, we enjoyed a few

moments of bliss, until a voice said: 'How would you like to come into my hut? I've a bag of sweets in there.'

Already, I was on my feet. Apples were one thing, sweets were quite another. I just could not resist the offer. The owner of the voice was a middle-aged man, older than my dad, with a pot belly and small, beady eyes, like two black beetles. He was mainly bald except for a few desperate wisps of hair.

'You can wait here,' he said, nodding at Deirdre. 'This way,' he said to me, showing me through the gates of a factory and into a small caretaker's hut. There was barely room, with the gardening tools and cleaning aids, for me to sit down. Without fuss, he turned the key in the door and pulled down the small blind at the window. He picked up a white paper bag and showed me the contents – delicious-looking strawberry-shaped sweets, dipped in icing sugar.

'Ooh,' I said, as my hand reached up, instinctively.

But the bag was snapped shut.

'First,' he said, nodding towards me, 'you need to do something for me. Then you can have a sweet.'

'Yes,' I nodded readily. 'Yes.'

I'd have jumped off the factory roof if it meant getting a sweet. In the next moment, his dark green trousers were around his knees.

'Come here,' he said to me. 'Be a good girl now.'

He took my small hand in his and began to groan softly as he moved it up and down his Thing.

Recoiling at the soft, rubbery skin, I mumbled: 'No, I don't like it. I don't like it.'

There was a rush in my throat as my mouth filled with a watery vomit and I had to close my eyes and swallow it back down again. My mind screamed at me to run away. Yet I felt almost paralysed; pinned into place, like a dead butterfly on a display board.

'Do you want a sweet?' he asked, an impatience in his voice now, which made me think there was only one answer he would accept.

'Yes,' I whispered, keeping my eyes tightly shut.

My only focus was those strawberry goodies, covered in sugar. I was moments away from tasting one myself. I clung onto that thought with my fingernails, as though I were hanging from a ledge. Yet it felt like hours later when he groaned more loudly, and my hand was suddenly and shockingly covered with a wet, sticky film. He wiped his own hand with a clean hanky from his pocket but didn't offer it to me. Instead, he held out the white paper bag and my heart lifted a little.

'Take one for your friend as well,' he said, and I thought to myself that he was very generous, that he wasn't so bad after all. But I was so eager, I automatically reached in with my right hand – the sticky hand. At once disgusted and delighted, I was dismayed by the lack of hygiene yet thrilled at the promise of the sweet.

'Thank you, mister, thank you,' I smiled as he opened the blind and unlatched the door.

'Next time you come, I'll have a penny for you,' he said, as I walked out into the too-bright sunshine where Deirdre was waiting on the bench.

The day felt brittle. Uncertain. All the way home, I concentrated on my sweet. Not on the man. Not on his rubbery Thing. Not on the sticky stuff. Those feelings were already parcelled up and buried, deep in my consciousness. Like the dust when

I was sweeping the floors at home, I wrapped them up in old newspaper and shoved them to the bottom of the outside bin. Deirdre and I didn't speak about it. She didn't ask me what had happened in that hut and I didn't once mention The Man or The Thing. We enjoyed our sweet, and if the taste was soured by what I had suffered, I pretended not to notice. A few days later, with hunger gnawing at my insides, I made my way, almost subconsciously, to the caretaker's hut. It was as though my legs had carried me there with a will all of their own.

'Come inside,' he said. 'I've a penny waiting here for you.'

Today, the air was thick with a malevolent miasma of sweat and alcohol, reminding me of dad's hangovers. The caretaker followed exactly the same routine as before, only this time I was wise enough to offer my left hand when accepting the penny.

'I'll be seeing you again soon,' he said confidently, as I hurried outside, clutching my penny like a prize. I did not see it then, but the way he dropped the latch and his trousers with such ease makes me sure he had done this kind of thing many times before. I certainly was not the first victim, nor would I be the last, and the thought fills me with anguish and anger. Worse still is the possibility that he had children and grandchildren of his own.

But I did not think of that then as I made my way to Sadie's sweet shop. The deliberation was wonderful. In 1968 there were so many sweets on offer for a penny or a halfpenny – Black Jacks, Fruit Salads, Refreshers, Mojos, Catherine Wheels, jelly snakes ... I took my time, and the decision was agonising and delightful in equal measure. I settled, eventually, on a regular penny chew. As the weeks passed, I returned time and time again to the caretaker, a decision which is on the one hand baffling and inexplicable, yet also entirely predictable. For I was being carefully groomed and exploited, with the pitiful promise of a sweet. It was a cheap reward, but it was the only one I ever got, and so I treasured it. The caretaker tended to stick to the same routine, requiring me to perform the same act at every visit.

He spoke very little, but one afternoon, he said to me, 'You have nice hair.'

I was surprised and pleased with the compliment. Nobody had ever noticed my hair before, not even my mother. Especially not my mother. Another time, he asked me to dance for him and, since we had no music, I had to make up a silly little song and twirl around as he watched. And while I felt awkward and out of place, I also felt special. Someone had noticed me, at last.

'You are so good at dancing,' he said, as he dropped his trademark green trousers.

And despite myself, I flushed with pride. Nobody had ever told me that I was good at anything. In a world where I was usually in trouble with the adults, this was a welcome change.

Another day, the caretaker announced he was changing the routine slightly, insisting I should use my own hand, without his to guide me.

'I can't,' I whimpered, sitting on my hands on a small stool behind the door. 'I can't do it on my own.'

'Well,' he replied, with a sad sigh. 'No penny for you, then.'

I could not bear the thought of leaving without my precious penny. It had become, in my mind, so much more than a single penny. So much more than a sweet. That penny had come to signify approval, affection and love. And though I didn't know it, these were gifts I longed for even more than sugar.

'OK,' I whispered, even though I was trembling, and my throat was tight with the threat of tears. I stood up and turned my head away as my hand reached towards the dreaded Thing. My stomach heaved as I moved my hand up and down, as I had been shown. I was telling myself this was just like doing the laundry or my schoolwork. I had a job to do, and it was best just to get on with it. But as his breathing grew more ragged, and I heard a familiar groan, the tears leaked out of my tightly closed eyes and streamed down my face.

'There's a good girl,' he grunted, as he pulled up his trousers. 'I've two pence for you today. What about that?'

His words were like a magic balm. Two pence! Two sweets! Or maybe a luxury macaroon. My hunger trumped all feelings of self-loathing. Sugar beat sensibility, every time.

'Thank you,' I smiled, as he fastened his belt.

I skipped out into the street, two consolation pennies in my hand, relieved that I had won his approval. I was a good girl, I reminded myself. A good girl. He had said so himself.

When school began again, I could not go to the factory as often, as it was a good walk away from our home. But I usually found time at the weekends, or maybe during the evenings. My parents never questioned where I was or who I was with. As long as I was on my knees in the living room at 6 p.m., ready for the Angelus, nothing else mattered. The bitter irony of that lives with me still. I did not look forward to visiting the care-taker at all but neither did I dread it. Those trips just became a part of my life. I learned to completely erase all thoughts from my consciousness, as though I was sweeping crumbs from a tabletop. By the time I walked out, into the daylight, my mind was completely blank. On the surface, I adopted a practical approach, and if this was what it took for me to have a sweet, then I was prepared to grit my teeth and see it through. There were several moments of utter revulsion, starting when he unzipped his trousers and ending when I got the penny in my hand. But as soon as I felt the coin in my palm, my thoughts switched effortlessly to the sweet shop so I was abused time and time again. The caretaker never once asked me to stay quiet. He did not threaten me or make me promise him anything. He did not use violence. And this distresses me almost more than the abuse itself. He must have known, by my grubby face, my well-worn clothes, my too-small shoes, that I was the perfect target. I could not have reported him for I did not have the confidence or the vocabulary to do so. And even if I had, nobody would have listened anyway. He did not silence me because he did not need to. Because I simply was not worth the hassle.

4

My maternal grandad lived in the same flats as my family, in the next block along. My grandmother had died when I was very small and I had only hazy memories of her floral overall, her red hair and her low, gentle voice. Grandad now lived alone, and so it was expected we would visit and keep him company every now and again. Grandad was a smart man who wore a suit jacket, waistcoat and shirt, no matter the occasion. He had a flat cap which he never removed, and as a small girl I wondered if he wore it in bed, too. I'd never seen him without it and had no idea if there was any hair lurking underneath. Grandad's flat was small and shabby, but on his window ledge he had an ornament of a brown and white dog, with big, sad eyes, which I loved to pat as I walked past. I enjoyed the calm and quiet of his home, in stark contrast to the chaos of my own. Grandad's front door had a flap attached which made a sound when it opened, and so there was no need to call out when I arrived. Always, I found him alone in the living room, either sitting straight or laid back and dozing. The visits with Grandad were usually uneventful; he might ask me about school, or we might just sit in silence.

But one day, around a year after the caretaker's abuse began, he said: 'I want you to do something for me and, after, I will give you a penny.'

As he unbuttoned his trousers, I was at once disgusted yet completely unfazed. Maybe, I reasoned, the caretaker knew my grandad and they'd agreed on a joint course of action. Perhaps the caretaker had been training me up for a new role with Grandad, and this was some sort of perverted promotion. Or it was possible they didn't know each other at all, and this was standard behaviour. This must be what all old men do, I told myself. It did not occur to me, aged nine, that my vulnerability marked me out like leprosy. I might as well have had a sign around my neck: 'This child has nobody looking after her.'

I had no thought that the abuse was wrong, that I was being failed and exploited in the worst way possible. Grandad made me hold his Thing, just as the caretaker had. His face was so close to mine, I could see the whiskers quivering on his chin, the sheen of sweat on his pale upper lip. Revulsed by the image, I closed my eyes. Afterwards, he handed me a penny.

'For the shop,' he said.

Again, just like the caretaker, there was no attempt from him to keep me quiet. He didn't tell me not to tell Mam, and he probably already knew I would not even consider confiding in her. She and I did not have that kind of bond. And anyway, I wasn't aware I had anything to tell. I didn't feel targeted or traumatised. I hated the abuse, but then I hated being belted by my father. I hated being hungry. I hated wearing smelly, urine-soaked clothes. This was just another injustice, on a long list, which I had to put up with. And the penny, of course, was the perfect salve. As soon as my small fingers closed around it, my thoughts turned to the delights of the sweet shop.

'Thank you, Grandad,' I said politely.

Despite the abuse or, possibly, heartbreakingly, because of it, the frequent visits to Grandad continued. I kept my mind fixed firmly on the end goal, the penny. To me, the abuse was no different from reciting the Angelus, where I was made to kneel on the hard floor until my knees hurt, with regular whacks from my father, but with the promise of a squeaky-clean soul and eternal salvation. Catholicism had made me an expert in shame and suffering. And if I felt hopeless and hurt that my own grandad was targeting me in the same way as a stranger, then I hid it deep down, at my core. I did not, could not, allow myself to consider it.

One day, after he had finished with me, Grandad fastened his trousers but he did not hand me the customary penny. Instead, he walked over to the stove, where an iron pot was simmering. Using a big spoon, he fished out a single boiled potato, small and a little slushy, and plopped it onto a tin plate.

'Here,' he said abruptly. 'I've no pennies. I'm not made of money you know. Make sure you bring the plate back later, good girl.'

I didn't dare question him, and instead stumbled outside, blowing at the potato to cool it down. Tragically, I was rather pleased with it. It was, after all, more substantial than a single sweet and it was evidence that I had won my grandad's approval. It wasn't long before my next visit, and this time, there was a coldness in my grandad's eyes and in his behaviour. A derision, a contempt. Without words, he made me feel as though I was completely without worth. When he handed me the penny, I shrank back, as though it was infected. I did not want it.

'Here,' he said gruffly, and I sensed his patience wearing thin.

'Thank you,' I said in a small voice, but as I curled my fingers around it, I felt the last vestiges of my self-esteem dredging away, like dirty water down a drain.

When I arrived home, my mother was standing at the sink, washing a big pan. With no planning, and with no intention, I shocked myself when I blurted out, 'Granda' makes me touch his Thing and I don't like it.'

I was not, in any way, reporting sexual abuse or even reporting my grandad for bad behaviour. I did not know if it was wrong or even what it was. But, like any other task, I did not like it. Maybe, deep down, there was a subconscious element of desperate self-preservation, hoping that my mother would listen to me and the abuse would be stopped. Instead, after I spoke, there was a long moment of silence, stretching like old chewing gum between us. My stomach lurched as I dug my nails into my palms. Already, I wanted to swallow those words back. The silence was more frightening than the explosion which followed. My mother suddenly spun around, soap suds flying, her face contorted with anger.

'I will box your ears if you keep on telling lies!' she hissed, and I ran from the house.

No doubt she did what she thought was best. She had her own problems, her own challenges, and over the years my anger dissipated into pity. The abuse from Grandad was less frequent than the caretaker's and it would come to an end just over a year later, when we moved away. Through it all, I had no conscious thoughts at all of trauma or suffering. I did not believe I was in any way damaged or distressed. And so, lacking the thought processes and the vocabulary to verbalise the abuse, and with no support for my pain, my suffering manifested as physical. After every stressful event, there was an equal bodily reaction. My seizures became worse and more frequent, and I passed out regularly at school. One day, after a particularly nasty bout of bullying, I had a seizure in the school playground. When I came round, I had a lump on the back of my head that was tender for weeks. Another day, at home, I was listening to my parents arguing, their voices growing louder and increasingly vicious, until I felt I could bear it no longer. Clapping my hands over my ears, I felt suddenly dizzy and sick, before falling to the floor, unconscious. When I came round, I was gagging on a spoon my mother was using to press my tongue down.

'You're fine now,' she said briskly.

Every time I was stressed, or scared, I'd sense a seizure coming on in the same way that other children might feel a sneeze. Sometimes, in the moments before the pain hit my head, I'd get a strong smell in my nostrils, as though I had my head in a bucket of tar. It was horrible. And despite my mother telling me they were nothing to worry about, I dreaded them. I hated those last few cloudy moments, when the walls and the ceiling seemed to crowd in on me, when my head thumped and my stomach roiled. As I came round, there was often a gaggle of bemused faces peering at me, either my classmates or my siblings.

I developed a stutter too and I could barely get through a sentence without sticking on single consonants. It was the worst luck that I struggled so much with 's' and so I was unable even to warn my teachers or my parents that I had a seizure coming.

'I'm having a s-s-s-s-' I tried.

Mostly, before I could formulate the word, everything went dark around me, and I fell into unconsciousness.

In class each day, children were picked at random by the nuns to read a passage from the Bible. Nobody enjoyed it, but for me it was a terrifying prospect. I was not a good reader, and I stumbled over some of the longer words. And my stutter didn't help one bit. The other children would laugh as soon as I was chosen, because they knew I would struggle and make a spectacle of myself. Each time I read, the stress became unbearable, and the room began to spin. When I came round, lying on the classroom floor, I'd see the fuzzy outline of a nun holding a plastic cup of water. Like the poverty and the smell of urine, the seizures and the stutter marked me out as different. Unwanted. Unworthy. Already a shy child, I became more withdrawn and solitary, retreating further and further into my shell and taking my secrets with me.

5

One freezing night, early in 1971, my father made an announcement.

'We're moving to England tomorrow,' he said. 'Get packing.'

The soup-like silence which followed was thick with unspoken questions. We were all, frankly, astonished. But we knew better than to show it. Moving house was not in itself unusual. We had moved five times, around the Dublin area, by the time I'd turned eleven that January. But a trip to England was another prospect entirely.

'What language do they speak?' asked one of the little ones. 'And will we have a bath? Will we have a telly?'

We had no suitcases or bags and so Mum instructed us to fill the old pram, which had carried each and every one of us, with as many clothes and belongings as we could squash in. It was arguably lucky, then, that we owned very little and the packing was soon done. I had nothing really to call my own – no toys, no books and just a few items of clothing that were shared with my sisters.

I didn't class Polly as a toy, she was more a member of the family, and I planned to carry her under my arm, as always, on the journey. We were going to live in Derby, my mother explained, where her brother and his family lived. My eyes widened at the prospect. She might just as well have said we were moving to Mars. I'd never been outside Dublin in my whole life. The furthest I'd been was those depressing seaside trips, battling downpours and dodgy windscreen wipers. For some reason, my eight siblings and I were travelling first with my mother, and my father would follow a few days later, in a yellow van he'd just acquired. The following evening, as we trooped down the stone steps from our home for the final time, the excitement was palpable.

'Do the English have lemonade on tap?' asked my little sister. 'And colour tellies? That's what I've heard.'

We walked to the bus stop, and I caught sight of Duke, our family dog, slinking down a side street.

'Can we take him?' I asked. 'Please? I can't leave him behind. I just can't.'

But my mother fixed me with an icy glare, and I knew not to speak again. But seeing his big brown eyes, liquid and sad, as we climbed aboard the bus without him, broke my heart. I have no idea what became of him or whether he survived, but I still think of him.

On the bus, Mam shooed us like a swarm of flies past the conductor and told him, 'I've only three halves to pay for, and myself please.'

It was the same when we got to the ferry. She managed to avoid paying for most of her children by herding us quickly past the barriers. It was an overnight crossing, and I slept on a wooden bench for the first few hours. When daylight came, I ran around on deck, searching, as always, for a dropped sweet or a lost penny. When I spotted a coin, underneath a bench, I was thrilled and instantly imagined the mouth-watering selection on offer inside Sadie's shop. But looking out across the grey and choppy waves, I realised with a jolt that there would be no more Sadie's. No more Jacko. No more Duke. My heart splintered when I thought of the friends I'd never see again and the games I'd never play. But the cold Irish Sea now tossed and rolled between me and my abusers, too. I was safe. The nightmare was over. I wish I could say I was triumphant, overcome with relief and joy that my torture at the hands of the caretaker and Grandad was at an end. But trauma is not so straightforward. As the coastline of North Wales loomed into view, and the seagulls squawked indignantly overhead, I felt torn and confused. Doubt slithered, snake-like, through my thoughts. No more caretaker. No more Grandad. No more monsters. No more pennies. No more sweets. This new country was exciting, but it was terrifying too. For as much as I loathed the abuse, it was all I knew.

'Come on,' my mother said crisply, hurrying us all down the gangplank ahead of the pram. 'We've a train to catch.'

On the station platform at Holyhead, I spotted a vending machine and, with my coin in my palm, I ran over to make a purchase. But after slotting in the money and making my choice, nothing happened.

'It's s-s-s-stolen my m-m-m-money,' I stammered.

'Oh, Kathleen, we've no time for this,' replied my mother, already shepherding the little ones into line ready for the train. It was pointless to make a fuss, but I felt the loss of my penny keenly. It seemed like a gross injustice, and a dark portent of what awaited us in this new and unfriendly country.

The train journey was long, and it was evening again by the time we arrived in Derby, cold, hungry and exhausted. It was snowing, soft flakes coming down thickly as we walked the last few miles of the journey. Mum wore a fake fur coat, which she'd picked up in a charity shop. But none of the children had coats, or even waterproof shoes. I was wearing a pair of PE pumps, given to me by a teacher, and my feet were soon soaked and aching with cold. The little ones grumbled and whimpered and Mum opened her coat so they could hide underneath, like baby chickens under her warm feathers. I did not go under the coat, much as I longed to. The walk felt endless as the city streets gave way to trees and fields and quieter suburbs. And then, in the distance, we spotted it. A large, detached house, with a garden and a farm behind it.

'Is that our new house?' I asked, a flush of anticipation warming my cheeks despite the temperature. 'It's massive!'

It looked bigger than the entire block of flats we'd left behind and I had no idea how my parents had afforded it. And it seemed we were expected here, too: there was furniture, a TV, and beds with blankets and pillows. There was even a fridge – the first time I'd ever seen one. In Dublin, we'd kept our milk fresh in cold water in the sink. Our new landlord had left a fire burning in the grate and we all crowded around gratefully to thaw out. Our belongings in the pram were soaked through, and Deirdre and I draped them around the room to dry. When the snow started, I had tucked Polly into the pram to keep her warm. But as I unpacked the last few items, there was no sign of her. I checked again and again, alarmed at the thought of Polly lying all alone on an English pavement.

'Have you seen Polly?' I asked my mother. 'Has anyone picked Polly up?'

But nobody had.

'You'll find another doll,' said Deirdre. 'Don't worry.'

But I didn't want another. I wanted my Polly. I worried, with her spiky hair and one leg, whether anyone else would want her. Nobody would ever love her as I had. When bedtime came, we took a small shovel of burning coal up to the fireplaces in the bedrooms. There were four bedrooms in total, and so I shared a double bed with just two of my sisters. The space was startling. For the first time in my life I could stretch out my legs without crashing head-on into another pair. But I longed to feel Polly's head next to mine on the pillow, her bristly hair scratching my cheek.

'This house is huge,' Deirdre whispered. 'And we've a garden. I like it here.'

'Me too,' I replied sleepily, but deep down, I wasn't sure that was the truth. I missed Duke. I missed Polly. And in spite of what I'd left behind, in spite of the horrors I'd escaped, the anxiety rose like a tide in my chest. Like the grime and dirt that clung to my skin, a film of unease and uncertainty wrapped itself around me. Perhaps it was me, I decided, as Deirdre fell into a deep, peaceful sleep. Perhaps it was all my fault. Poor Polly was lost. And in my own way, I felt lost too. Worse, I felt responsible. I had brought all of this on myself, by taking money from old men. Yes, maybe that was it. Maybe I was the bad penny, in every sense of the word.

Dad arrived in his yellow van a couple of days later and, the following week, I enrolled at the local school. As in Ireland, my grey uniform came from a charity shop and was tatty and ill-fitting. My mother tutted at the skirt hanging low on my waist, as though it was my fault I was so thin. I was wary of starting at a new school, in a new country, and I was right to be. For from that first day, I was the target of relentless and racist bullying. These days, it seems, everyone is only too happy to claim a portion of Irish heritage. Back then, it was quite the opposite. Following the introduction of the Race Relations Act three years earlier, attitudes were changing, but oh so slowly. And some took longer than others. My mother reported seeing signs on village shops and in the windows of hotels and pubs: 'No Blacks, No Irish, No Dogs.' By now, we had a new dog, Major, so we were doubly unpopular. And in the school playground, it was even worse. Many times since, I have thought that a school yard can be the cruellest and loneliest place in the world.

'Kathleen Ryan-ocerous!' chanted the other kids. 'You smell like the zoo! You stink like a Ryan-ocerous!'

They presumed, with no evidence whatsoever, that I was an IRA member, and each time I walked past, they made shooting or bombing sounds. Every time I put my bag down, they jumped back, screaming in delight that I was carrying explosives.

'Are you bringing a bomb to school tomorrow?' they asked. 'Are you going to blow us up, Irish?'

Strange as it might seem, I'd never heard of the IRA. I only ever watched the Angelus on TV, and I had no access to newspapers or radio. My upbringing, though in a big city, had been remarkably insular. Irish current affairs were a bigger deal for me in Derby than they ever had been in Dublin. But whenever I opened my mouth to explain, the other kids would either burst out laughing or feign complete ignorance at what I was trying to say.

'P-p-p...'

It was hopeless. The harder I tried, the more I stuttered.

'P-lease l-l-leave me al-l-one.'

'What language is that?' they asked, screwing up their faces. 'Can't understand a word you say, Irish.'

My stutter got so bad that I stopped speaking altogether. There were some school days when I just didn't open my mouth at all. The teachers sat me at the back of the class and, as long as I was quiet, they didn't bother me. I was an outsider, an intruder, in every way. I soon realised that my Irish education lagged way behind the English system, and I couldn't follow most of the lessons. I was too embarrassed to ask for help in school, and it was pointless to do so at home. Dad was completely illiterate, having had no education himself. Mam could read and write, but said she was too busy to help with my homework. Late one night, I was busy at the kitchen table struggling with my maths when a large rat scuttled across the skirting board. I screamed so loudly that Dad came blundering downstairs, hit me hard and ripped up my homework. The rat, as far as I know, got away without punishment, but I was handed a detention the next day. Not long after arriving in Derby, I conceded that school was simply not for me. Even in my first year of secondary school, I was so far behind I knew I could never catch up. I could do nothing about my lack of education. But I was determined to do something about the smell. Even though our new home had a fancy top-loading washing machine, Mam often didn't have time to use it and so I got to grips with the instructions and began a daily laundry routine. But though I was older now, nearly twelve years of age, there was still occasional bed-wetting, triggered by anxiety. And there were so few clothes to go round that it was impossible to guarantee a clean uniform. I came up with a cunning plan of spreading my school shirt and skirt under the mattress each night, where nobody else would see it. My idea had the twofold advantage of flattening and hiding the outfit at the same time. And it gave me great pleasure, lying in bed with my sisters, knowing they were oblivious to my invention. The next morning, my clothes appeared freshly ironed. But no matter what I did, and how much I cleaned and washed, the bullying continued. And the more I tried to fit in, the more, conversely, I stood out.

'Ryanocerous, get back to the zoo!' screamed the kids, holding their noses and laughing, as though it was the greatest joke ever.

'Don't go near her, she's got a bomb! And don't speak to her because she can't speak back!'

The move to Derby did not seem to suit my parents, either, and they argued constantly. Often, late at night, I'd hear them yelling at each other through the walls. Mainly, they rowed about money. Even though we seemed to have a little more cash these days, it was never enough. One evening, Dad ordered us all upstairs and, as we hung over the banister, we were alarmed to hear paramedics carrying my mother outside into an ambulance.

'He's killed her,' whispered my brother. 'They've been arguing and now Mam is dead.'

Later we were all still slumped on the floorboards, sobbing, when Dad stuck his face around the corner of the landing.

'Kathleen.' He pointed at me. 'You come with me to the hospital. The rest of you, behave.'

Still under the impression that Mam was dead, or at the very least dying, I trembled with fear as I climbed into the yellow van. It was my job, as usual, to shout out the road signs and the directions, and it took all my literacy skills to navigate our way through a strange city. It was only when Dad said, 'Look out for Maternity signs,' that I realised my terrible misunderstanding. Mam wasn't injured or dead at all, she'd had a baby! She'd been hiding another secret under her big apron, and nobody had guessed. My baby brother, her tenth child, was beautiful. I was mesmerised, leaning into the cot, stroking his soft cheeks and marvelling at his pink starfish hands.

'Jesus,' said Dad, as he sat down heavily on a chair. 'No more kids. This is it now.'

My mother shot him a look. 'It's not me, it's you,' she protested. 'You have to leave me alone.'

Dad chose one name for the new baby, she chose another, but Mam got her way. And I understood, as we drove home, that Mam made many of the important decisions in our family. Dad had the loudest voice and the worst temper. But that did not tell the whole story. Perhaps this was the way in many families.

6

Busy with a new baby and lacking the community support she'd had back home, Mam spent hours scanning the classified ads in the local paper, looking for cheap baby clothes or items of furniture. Over time, she began trading. She'd bid for old gas cookers, clean them up and sell them on for a profit. It was a gem of a business idea. The only problem was, I was required to call the seller from the local phone box to put in the bid.

'Nothing to it, Kathleen,' my mother said. 'Just offer them half price and see what they say. You need to haggle.'

That first time, my jaw dropped in a mix of disbelief and fear. She might just as well have asked me to run a marathon backwards. I was already painfully quiet and shy, and my stutter made me reluctant to speak to anyone at all, let alone a complete stranger, on the telephone.

'Come on,' she said impatiently, holding out the newspaper.

Her request encompassed every nightmare I'd ever had, all

rolled into one. But I dared not refuse. With the newspaper under my arm and a 2-pence coin in my hand, I set off for the red phone box on the corner. By the time I arrived, the knot of fear in my stomach was unravelling rapidly and snaking down to my fingers and toes.

'Do not stutter,' I ordered myself firmly. 'Do. Not. Stutter.'

But I might as well have tried to stop breathing. The moment the seller answered, I was overcome with a dizzying panic.

'Hel-hel-hel-' I stuttered.

The lady on the other end waited patiently for a few seconds, but she quickly became concerned.

'What are you trying to say?' she asked. 'Is it help? Do you need help? Is that it? Are you in danger?'

'Hel-' I said again.

'Do you need the police?' she asked. 'Or an ambulance? Are you hurt?'

This was disastrous. I tried shaking my head but, of course, she couldn't see that. The only way I could stop my stutter was to give myself a sharp kick and then shout at the top of my voice. It was a tried and tested method, and it always worked. I took a moment, filled my lungs, kicked my own leg and yelled, 'Hel-lo!' as loudly as I could.

There was a stunned silence. She must have thought me extremely rude. Then just as I was preparing to shout out my enquiry, the pips sounded and my money ran out. The call had ended without me even placing my bid. I had no choice but to traipse back home with a bruise on my leg to face my mother's wrath.

'You'll have to take another two pence and try again,' she said crossly. 'I want that cooker, Kathleen.'

And so it all began again. Mam knew about my stutter so I have no idea why she selected me, out of her ten children, to make the phone calls. Maybe she thought the speaking practice would do me good – kill or cure. But there were times when I came home in tears, frustrated, embarrassed and ashamed by my own inadequacies. And any punishment from my mother just made my stutter worse. I used to dread being sent to the phone box. It was like facing a firing squad. Now, with my stutter a distant memory, I can't help but chuckle when I think of all those households I rang, pleading hel-hel-hel-, before screaming like a banshee. I never once managed to tell them why I was calling. Even now, I'm not one for going after a bargain. I find the stress outweighs the prize.

One day in spring, as the weather was warming up, Dad announced he was giving up smoking. This was something of a double-edged sword because, while I could breathe easier in the house, he was even more bad-tempered and irritable than usual. One sunny afternoon, he sent me out to buy a block of ice cream. I was so excited, I practically danced down the pavements to the local shops. One block would not go far among twelve of us, I told myself in an attempt to temper my enthusiasm. But just a small taste would be lovely. I hadn't had any ice cream since those days when I was trusted to look after the ice-cream van, while Dad was off claiming his dole.

'Oh, you'll enjoy this,' smiled the shopkeeper as he handed me my change and the carrier bag of ice cream.

On the way home, I hugged the bag to me like a baby and ran as fast as I could, before it melted. When I got in, Dad was already waiting at the table with an upright spoon in his hand.

He said nothing, but took the ice cream, peeled back the cardboard and began to eat. Spoonful by spoonful, the block grew smaller and smaller, and my heart seemed to shrivel at the same pace. Soon it was all gone, and he looked up enquiringly.

'I need ice cream, I'm giving up smoking,' he said, licking his lips.

My reward for my trip to the shop was to be allowed to lick the cardboard clean. I wish I could say I threw it back in his cruel face. But like a stray dog, I was grateful for any morsel, any treat at all, that was thrown my way. And though it tasted of nothing but wet cardboard, I licked the packaging until it disintegrated in my hands.

Another day, Dad had a bag of chocolate drops, which he was scoffing two or three at a time. Nobody dared ask him for a sweet. But he must have sensed a crowd of children following him from room to room, as if he were the Pied Piper.

'I cannot offer you one,' he said, as he popped another in his mouth. 'I need these sweets because I am giving up smoking.'

It will probably not surprise you to learn that he smoked until the day he died decades later.

In Derby, we had more available food than in Ireland. There were no treats; the ice cream and sweets were limited only to my father. I was desperate to fit in at school and now understood that scraping chewing gum off the pavement, or searching through bins, was socially unacceptable and was not the best way to make friends. And so for many weeks, I had no sweets at all. While it was a relief, certainly, that the abuse was at an end, I missed the regular pennies and the trips to Sadie's. Looking back, I'm dismayed at how forcefully I dismissed the childhood abuse from my consciousness. I never confided in anyone – not even, crucially, myself. I didn't know how. Instead, I took all the bad memories, threw them in the deepest sink hole and told myself that was the end of them. I knew no other way. The abuse had stopped, the pennies had stopped and I simply had to erase both from my mind. But though treats were in short supply in Derby, there was usually a meal ready after school, a stew or a pie, or at least a loaf of bread for toast. There was a strict hierarchy in the household, which had little to do with money and more to do with control. We were not allowed to open the press, as we called the kitchen cupboard, to help ourselves. Mam was in charge of all that and she apportioned food according to status. Dad had butter; we had margarine. At weekends, my parents had steak while the children were allowed a single sausage each. I loved to help Mam make the gravy for the steak. Dutifully, I sliced mushrooms and onions, knowing I'd never get to taste them, but enjoying the task regardless. Always, I was looking for recognition – a pat on the back, a thank you, a compliment from my mother. Always, I was hoping for her love. As with the caretaker and my grandad, my greatest fear was to let her down and disappoint her. Her approval, like theirs, was of life-affirming importance to me.

At school, unlike in Ireland, we had free dinners, including pudding, which was usually semolina. I didn't care what it was, how runny or how lumpy, I devoured the lot. Dinner time was the only enjoyable part of the school day. And it was while sitting in the dining hall that I finally began to make friends. Sally could not, superficially, have been more different to me. She wore a pristine uniform and her hair was neatly brushed and curled. Her shoes shone and her navy-blue school bag matched her warm woollen coat. Her devoted parents drove her to and from school each day. As we stirred our semolina, I gazed at her with a sense of wonder, tinged with envy. I'd never met anyone so impossibly perfect. And yet, she had a lovely nature – open and warm. Sally was in the Girls' Brigade, and she suggested I might like to join up.

'Oh, yes please,' I beamed.

My parents had no objections as long as no money or effort was required from them. I loved going to the brigade each week, wearing a hand-me-down uniform with its jaunty peaked hat. I joined the band, too, playing a borrowed trumpet. I hadn't a clue how to read music or play an instrument, but I was so pleased to be included that I just stood at the back of the hall and pretended to play, putting the instrument to my lips and wiggling my fingers without blowing a single note. I used to marvel that not one of the guides had ever found me out. But looking back, I'm sure they realised exactly what was going on and left me to it. I was even allowed to perform at shows, with the rest of the band, again not playing a single sound. I took such pride in my uniform and my trumpet, and they were happy times. Understanding and not complaining that she could not come to my house, Sally invited me round for tea, where, in the centre of a polished oval dining table, was a big bowl filled with oranges, apples, pears and bananas. Seeing the shiny red apples reminded me of the fruit Deirdre and I had stolen that first time I'd been ambushed by the caretaker, and I reddened with shame. Those days were behind me now, I reminded myself.

'Would you like a banana sandwich?' asked Sally's mother, picking two bananas out of the bowl. 'With sugar on top? And a glass of lemonade each?'

Rendered temporarily speechless, I nodded. I'd never had a banana before, or any kind of fizzy drink.

'It's delicious,' I said, as I tasted the first mouthful. 'Really tasty. Thank you. Thank you.'

I said it so often that Sally's mother took my face in her hands and smiled. 'You're welcome, my love,' she beamed. 'Fill yourself up. There's plenty.'

The shelves on Sally's bedroom walls were lined with about thirty dolls from around the world.

'Look, here's one from Ireland,' she said, smiling. 'I'm going to call her Kathy.'

I was so honoured that I found myself, inexplicably, wiping away a solitary tear. Sally was almost like a doll herself, and I could imagine her standing in line with the others with her beautiful skin, her neatly brushed hair, her clean, fresh clothes. Her life was so far away from what I was used to that she just did not seem real. I thought of my own lost doll, Polly, with her missing leg and her awful scratchy hair, and realised, with some sadness, that she and I had been perfectly matched. I'd loved her, despite all her shortcomings. Another friend, Marie, had Irish parents and we bonded over our shared background. When Marie invited me round, we'd get comfy on her big sofa, bolstered on all sides by cushions, and talk for hours. Her mother made chip butties for us and brought in big jugs of cordial.

'You two girls can talk the hind legs off a donkey,' she laughed.

Strangely, with Marie, I never stuttered. Not once. I didn't understand why back then. But at her home, and in her company, I felt accepted. I felt safe and secure. I loved visiting my friends, but going home each time, I always felt empty and slightly jealous. I would have given anything for one of their luxuries – the loving mother, the benevolent father, the tasty suppers, the collection of dolls, the beautiful clothes. How was it that they had everything and I had nothing?

A voice inside me, cold, contemptuous and dripping with judgement, had the answer: *You're not good enough, Kathleen. You're not at their level and you never will be. You're not worth the same as them.*

And as much as I tried to shake this thought, like a wasp buzzing around my head, it refused to leave me.

7

I made new friends outside school, too. Opposite our new home there was a big building with a stream of children coming in and out. One afternoon my curiosity got the better of me and I went to peer in through the windows. The place looked like a holiday camp. There was a table tennis match in full swing and a big stage, where children were singing and dancing. I could hear music and laughter. Then the main door opened, and a man beckoned me inside.

'Come on,' he smiled. 'Would you like to join in at Sunshine Corner?'

'Oh yes,' I said shyly. 'Yes, please.'

I played table tennis for the first time in my life and even allowed myself to be persuaded onto the stage to dance with the other kids.

When it was time for home, the man said to me: 'You can come back next time if you like? Every Tuesday and Thursday, and it's completely free.'

My smile lasted all the way home. After that first day, I never missed a chance to go to the club. The owner often sang on the stage himself and the helpers gave out little bags of blackjack sweets. I made lots of good friends, and my siblings and cousins often came along too. Our six cousins lived on the next street to us, only a five-minute walk away, so I saw them a lot. There were two boys and four girls, ranging in age from five to sixteen, and we all got on well. We had such fun at Sunshine Corner; it was the nearest I ever got to a mini holiday. I could not think of a more appropriate name for the place – it was indeed a little corner of sunshine.

That first summer, the club organised a trip to Markeaton Park in Derby, and I took a letter with the details home for our mother, bursting with the excitement of a proper outing. There was a boating lake and a cafe and a paddling pool at the park, and my imagination ran riot with the promise of ice creams and sandcastles and hide and seek. When the day came around, I was outside the club early in the morning, ready with my summer clothes and a big smile. But as I got to the front of the bus queue, the lady in charge said: 'Sorry, you haven't paid. You can't come, Kathleen, if your mother hasn't paid.'

My mother, who was waiting nearby, simply shrugged and nodded in the direction of home. I watched tearfully from the living-room window as the bus trundled past without me, carrying all the other children to the park. But I was sad only in that transitory childish way and soon I was off out to play with my brothers and sisters. All thoughts of the boating lake forgotten, we built a den perilously close to the railway line, so that the walls of old planks and a discarded tarpaulin shuddered whenever a train went past. It was probably very dangerous, but then that was half the attraction. My designated job, of course, was cleaner, and I took great pride in sweeping the floor and tidying. As the weeks passed, we gathered odd stuff and hid it in there as though it was treasure. A scarf. An old tyre. A half bottle of cherryade. I loved going to the den, having something secret and separate from my parents.

But the best thing by far about living in Derby was a teacher named Diane. She was Deirdre's teacher but seemed to take a shine to us both. No doubt she noticed the pungent smell, the second-hand clothes, that lost, wayward, look we had, like little orphaned rabbits. It turned many teachers away, but it drew her towards us. One day at breaktime, she announced that in the summer holidays she was getting married, and wondered would we like to attend?

Before I could point out the obvious, she added: 'I've picked out dresses and shoes for you both. Would you like to see them?'

The pink dresses, with extravagant front bows, were like something out of a storybook. When I tried on the white shoes, I felt like one of the dolls lined up on Sally's bedroom shelf. Impossibly perfect.

'Well?' she asked. 'Would you like to come?'

As if it was ever in doubt! Diane cleverly framed the idea to my mother that she needed drinks servers at her reception. Mam always liked the idea of us pitching in with manual work and earning our living. It was agreed Diane would arrange for us to be collected in a posh black car on the morning of the wedding and returned back home the following day. The wedding ceremony and reception was like a real-life fairy tale and as Deirdre and I floated around, handing out drinks and tasting elegant little sandwiches from the buffet, we felt like princesses. It was as though we'd been plucked out of our humdrum existence by our very own fairy godmother. The problem with being Cinderella, of course, is that it doesn't last. And after a night at the hotel – the first time in my life I'd ever had my own bed – it was time to go home. But I knew I'd never forget Diane and the kindness she showed us. In years to come, when I was drowning in darkness and despair, I'd remind myself of her generosity and I'd remember that someone cared.

One year in, and we were all settling well in Derby. Mam got a job cleaning at a Scholl shoe shop in the town centre. Every day after school, I went along to help. As I swept, Mam followed me with the mop. While I took the bins out, Mam bleached the toilets. I loved cleaning but, more than that, I loved spending that time with her. I hoped the synchronicity of our tasks might somehow bring us closer together. I wanted us to feel like a team, a unit, a mother and daughter. Yet the more I looked for that feeling, the more I tried to force that bond, the further it seemed to slip away. Though she might be standing right next to me with a cleaning rag in her hand, my mother felt distant and unreachable. Those evenings of cleaning were perfectly pleasant. But I wanted more from her. Whatever precious yet intangible sentiment I craved, it simply was not there.

Dad was working as a scaffolder and, most mornings, his pickup truck failed to start. As soon as we heard his engine cough we were expected to run outside, without prompting, to give it a push. One morning, as I leaned my weight into the truck, I felt dizzy and sickly, and the truck seemed to fall backwards on me. When I woke, I was lying on the wet gravel, my siblings staring down at me.

'She's had another seizure,' someone shouted.

I was carted unceremoniously into the house and left in a heap on the kitchen floor, while the rest of the family got the truck going.

Afterwards, as Mam rinsed her hands under the tap, she said, 'Kathleen, get up now, you're going to be late for school.'

Having just suffered a blackout seizure, I walked the mile and a half to school without even questioning the harshness of the decision to myself, because I knew no different.

Most Sundays, we went to Mass. Dad never attended church, and neither would he agree to drive us there. Instead, as with school, we had to walk the whole way, passing by his truck but not passing comment. Everyone understood that Dad was not to be challenged. And so when he announced one evening that we were leaving Derby, I was careful not to react. But immediately I thought of my new friends, of Diane, of the den, of the Girls' Brigade, of the wonderful Sunshine Corner. I had only just found a little scrap of happiness and now it was to be snatched from under me. We were moving to Gloucester, Dad explained, where Mum had another brother.

'Gloucester! Where is that?' asked Sally, when I broke the news the next morning at school.

'No idea,' I replied glumly. 'But we're leaving tonight.'

I didn't understand why we always had to move, whether we were running because of debt, habit or pure old-fashioned wanderlust. It was not my place to ask. Gloucester was around a two-hour drive away. Crammed into the back of Dad's van in a disorderly pile were ten children, dozens of carrier bags stuffed with clothes and belongings, a television and four mattresses. There was barely space to breathe.

Yet as the engine revved, Dad drummed his fingers on the side of the van and shouted: 'Sing! I want to hear you singing!'

In a small voice, I began. 'Daddy's taking us to Gloucester today, Gloucester today, Gloucester today.'

The others joined in and somehow, as the journey got underway, I began to feel genuinely curious and excited about our new home. Hopefully, there would be a Sunshine Corner there too.

My parents had bought the house in Gloucester, a two-bedroom terrace, and it was much smaller than our rented place in Derby. We were back to being jammed in together on sofas and in beds. My heart sank when I realised I'd be sharing a bed with the little ones, once again trying to mask the smell of bed-wetting. There was no washing machine in the new house, either. In the girls' bedroom there were two large double beds which took up all the space. There was no room for a wardrobe, or even a set of drawers, and instead our clothes were piled up on the floor in one big smelly mess. The boys had the other bedroom and my parents slept downstairs. One of my brothers, Danny, immediately railed against the new living arrangements and slept in an armchair for two weeks, before announcing he'd found a job and was leaving home. But still, space was tight. Dad was handy around the house, and he decided to move the whole bathroom downstairs so he could create another bedroom upstairs. I was roped in to help carry the bath down the narrow staircase. And afterwards, I was required to pass screwdrivers, saws and spirit levels to Dad as he worked. If I selected the wrong tool, he'd clatter me over the head with it and so I soon learned to distinguish a spanner from a wrench.

I started at yet another new school, with new faces, new

taunts, new bullies. And though I'd seen and heard it all before, it bothered me just the same. This time, however, the new cousins were around my age, and so I at least had ready-made friends and allies. And I surprised myself by settling in and making new friends more quickly than I'd expected.

8

We had been in Gloucester less than a year when I came home one day to find Dad had gone.

'We've split up,' Mam explained. 'He's left.'

He hadn't even said goodbye but, in all honesty, I felt mostly relieved. I did not miss those drumming fingers and that volcanic temper. Mam announced we were moving back to Dublin, nearer to friends and family. By now, the older ones had moved out, meaning I was the eldest at home.

'You'll have to get a full-time job,' she told me. 'We need the money.'

At thirteen, I was very pleased to leave school. I'd never really enjoyed studying. We moved into two rented rooms just opposite our old home in Dublin, and Aunty Frances called in to say she'd heard of jobs going at the local coat factory.

'I'll take you round there, if you like,' she suggested. 'Let me do the talking.'

The boss showed us in and asked me, 'How old are you?'

'Fifteen,' Frances replied immediately. 'She's a good worker and she can start tomorrow.'

A few minutes later, I walked out of the factory with the job, without even having opened my mouth!

The next morning, Mam woke me while it was still dark and I left home, without breakfast, to start the half-hour walk to work. Arriving at the gates, I worried I'd be the youngest there. But in the crowd there were plenty of teenage faces, who'd obviously fibbed their way through the interview process as I had. I felt a ripple of excitement as I merged in with the chatter. At thirteen, I felt grown-up and adult. But walking past the ubiquitous caretaker's hut, much larger than the one I'd known and with a little chimney on the side, my legs wobbled a little. Suddenly sickly and nauseous, I was dragged back in time. I heard the latch drop, I smelled that mix of stale booze and sweat, I recoiled at the clammy and rubbery feel of the Thing. In that instant, it was like I was back there. And though I was miles away from him, on the other side of the city, I felt so scared and vulnerable. Not so grown-up after all. As I hung up my jacket and bag, a voice at my shoulder pulled me back to reality.

'Kathleen, is it?' asked a woman in her early twenties. 'You'll be working with me. I'm Aileen.'

Aileen showed me into a huge warehouse with row after row of sewing machines. The clanking of the machinery almost drowned out the radio belting out David Bowie and the Rolling Stones. It was my job, as a clipper, to cut any stray threads from the brightly coloured macs that hung on rails down the sides of the room. I thoroughly enjoyed this, humming away to 'Starman' and dreamily picking out the macs I liked while I clipped away with my scissors. I was also expected to press creases into the coats using a Hoffman presser, a type of huge ironing machine. But I was so small and skinny, and the machine was so heavy and clunky, I could barely lift the lid.

'Let me help you,' Aileen said under her breath. 'Before the boss sees you.'

At lunchtime, we went into the canteen and I took my place on a bench next to Aileen. She got her sandwiches out of her bag and began to eat.

'Where's yours?' she asked.

I shrugged.

'Here,' she smiled, handing me a jam sandwich. 'I've too many anyway.'

We ate in silence for a while and then she said: 'There's no way you're fifteen. I saw the way you struggled to lift that presser. I won't tell anyone, I promise.'

I liked Aileen, she seemed so kind, but I was too scared to confide in her. I couldn't afford to lose my job.

'I'm fifteen, really I am,' I protested.

As the weeks passed, I settled in well at the coat factory, far better than I ever had at school. I enjoyed the camaraderie and the craic. I loved the notion that I'd left my miserable childhood behind; it really did seem that simple. Every Friday, the brown paper envelope containing my wages went straight to Mam. I didn't get a single penny. And in the evenings, I was expected to clean and cook and wash at home, the same as always. Financially, it was harder now, without Dad around. But still, I didn't miss him one bit.

One weekend, Mam asked me to call in at Grandad's with some shopping. He was only a short walk away from our new flat. For a moment, I hesitated, but I couldn't think of an excuse not to go. Even now, aged thirteen, I had no words for what he had done. Pushing open the door, hearing the noisy flap, seeing the brown and white dog ornament, I was transported right back to being nine years old. Yet that was as far as it went. I cut off my thoughts as surely as if I'd sliced through them with a scalpel.

'Hello, Kathleen,' he beamed, when I walked into the living room. 'You've grown so much! Let me look at you.'

He was as friendly and at ease as if nothing had ever happened. In my confusion, I began to question myself. Did it happen? And, if it did, perhaps I was making a big fuss about nothing. Maybe sexual abuse was like a silly quarrel or a bump on the head. It was better not to dwell on it. Best not to make a big deal.

'I'll call in again soon,' I promised him.

Neither of us ever raised the issue of the abuse. Like a spectre, it hovered at the edges of my consciousness, a cobweb brushing against the walls of my mind. But I did not, could not, allow those notions to solidify into real thoughts. Instead, after each visit, I returned home and scrubbed the floors, washed the windows and polished the brasses. I cleaned until my hands were red and raw and until the surfaces shone. And yet it was never enough. My secrets were always there, like crocodiles lurking just beneath the water line.

A couple of years later, I got news that my grandad had died, and I burst into tears. Inexplicably, I felt genuine loss and grief. I missed him. For though he was my abuser, he was also my grandad. And it is this that makes abuse so difficult to deal with. The lines are blurred; the feelings are conflicting and confusing. I was bonded to my grandad by trauma. But also by love.

*

Shortly before my sixteenth birthday, Mam announced we were on the move again, back to Gloucester. She and Dad were apparently getting back together. Again, the move had come at a bad time for me. I enjoyed my job at the coat factory, and I'd made plenty of friends. I would have been perfectly content to stay in Dublin on my own, with Aunty Frances nearby for support. And I did not relish at all the prospect of seeing my father again. But Mam was counting on my wage, and she needed my help around the house, too. I felt a duty to help. More than that, I yearned, still, for her approval. It was like reaching for a star – no matter how far I stretched, I knew I'd never get there. Yet that didn't stop me trying, and the fact that I was needed by her was enough. Dad had already found us a terraced house near the centre of Gloucester, and I got a casual job in an off-licence on the same street.

A few weeks later, I was offered work at Wall's ice-cream factory. There was a huge advert on the factory wall: 'Go on . . . treat yourself!' It was my job to pack choc ices into boxes on a conveyor belt. As with the coat factory, I was in a huge room alongside hundreds of other girls and women. It was back-breaking work, standing in the same position all day, but it helped that we were all in it together. Along with the choc ices, we'd pass jokes and gripes and giggles down the conveyor belt, so that my shift usually flew by. The best part, by far, was helping ourselves to as much ice cream as we could eat when the supervisor's back was turned. As soon as he took a break, we'd unwrap a choc ice each.

'Go on . . . treat yourself!' we giggled.

Just as I was licking my lips, the lookout girl nearest the door would shout, 'Quick, he's coming back!' and we'd check each other's faces for smudges of chocolate, or telltale wrappers poking out of our pockets. I'd remember Dad scoffing a whole block of ice cream to himself, without sharing so much as a spoonful, and this felt like sweet, sweet justice on every level.

We hadn't been in Gloucester for more than a couple of months when Deirdre, then seventeen, moved back into the family home after a short spell living in her own place nearby. In hushed whispers, she confided that she was pregnant.

'I'm on my own,' she told me. 'What am I going to do? How will I look after a baby?'

I wasn't too worried about that. Deirdre had always been thoughtful and kind, and I knew she'd make a wonderful mother. But I was wary of our parents' reaction. At first, though, they seemed to take the news quite well. Deirdre sailed through her pregnancy and when her baby boy was born, we all idolised him. Deirdre had a carry cot by the bed, but he was never in it because there was always someone to carry him around and give him a cuddle.

He was only a few weeks old when my mother said: 'Deirdre, you're going to have to go, and take the baby with you. Your father doesn't like the noise.'

As we gasped, open-mouthed, she turned to me and added, 'You can go, too.'

'Why me?' I spluttered. 'I don't have a baby!'

'She'll need you to help her and look after her,' Mam replied curtly. 'Get your stuff packed up.'

I knew there was no point in arguing. But I felt horribly wronged. It was as though they had been looking for a chance to throw me out and get rid of me. Unbidden, images of the caretaker's hands and those bottle-green trousers flashed across my mind. The feel of the Thing, the rubbery squishiness, was as real and repulsive now as it had been when I was eight years old. I was worthless, I reminded myself. I was no good for anything. Even my own parents didn't want me. We had very few belongings and, with one carrier bag each, Deirdre and I were soon ready to leave.

'Let me know when you find a place,' said Mam, a tinge of regret in her voice.

I knew it was Dad's decision, not hers. But I felt a swell of resentment against her for not speaking up for us. Moments later, we were standing in the November drizzle with a rickety pram and two carrier bags.

'We have nowhere to go,' I said flatly. The dismay dampened my spirits even more than the rain.

But Deirdre smiled, and said: 'I've heard the Wests have a spare room. I have my social security money; you have your wages. Don't worry, Kathy, we'll be all right. It was horrible living with Mam and Dad anyway.'

The Wests lived just a five-minute walk away across the park and were well known locally for letting out rooms. Mr West was a handyman. I'd seen him around once or twice, doing jobs for our neighbours. Though I didn't know him, I knew the family name. Everyone did. Deirdre was always so sociable and chatty, and it was typical of her to know there were rooms for rent.

'Let's try there,' I agreed, and I suddenly felt a whole lot better.

9

The weather brightened as we crossed the park, past a grand statue of Robert Raikes, who had founded the Sunday School Movement. We continued, past a church and a corner shop and onto Cromwell Street. I was wearing my favourite blue T-shirt, and I took off my jacket and tied it round my waist, enjoying the warmth of the late-autumn sunshine on my arms. The Wests lived at number 25, next door to another church, in a semi-detached which had been extended at the back and so was bigger than the other houses. It was a plain, anonymous sort of place, rendered in a dull concrete colour with a neat fence at the front. On the wall was an ironwork sign printed in fancy curls: '25 Cromwell Street'. The sash windows were hung with clean net curtains. The black rubbish bin was full, the lid balanced precariously on the top. It was a typical family home. Yet as we waited on the side path for the door to open, my stomach churned with nerves. I had no idea what to expect. What if they sent us away? Where would we go? And though a part of me was relieved to escape the hardships at home, I was wary of living with a family of complete strangers. Better the devil you know.

'Can I help you, girlies?' asked a dark-haired man with a friendly face and a rich West Country accent.

When we explained we were looking for a room, he showed us into the hallway, where Deirdre parked the pram. Stepping into the living room on the left of the hallway was a little like rewinding back to my childhood in Dublin. There were kids and teenagers everywhere. They spilled off the sofa, perched on the arms and spread right across the carpet. There were children giggling, squabbling and whispering. And all of this while the TV in the corner competed for air space. And though the room was messy and chaotic, it was, crucially for me, quite clean. It was light and bright, too, thanks to a large window looking out over the back garden. Reassured and relieved, I allowed myself to breathe out a little. This was exactly what I was used to.

The man grinned at us and said, 'I'm Fred West.'

He had a wide, fleshy face, crooked teeth and lots of thick, dark brown hair, which crept in spidery sideburns down his cheeks. He looked about the same age as my dad. Most importantly, he seemed perfectly approachable and normal. I had a feeling we'd be safe here with him.

'Now, this is my wife, Rosemary,' Fred continued.

Rosemary was a different matter. She glanced sideways at us from her armchair against the right wall, but didn't smile. She too had dark hair, with sallow skin and heavy-lidded brown eyes behind large glasses. She looked much younger than Fred and was quite overweight. Possibly she was pregnant, but I couldn't be sure.

'And this,' said Fred, with a little half-turn towards a teenage girl, 'is my lover, Shirley.'

KATHLEEN RICHARDS with ANN CUSACK

I expected everyone to laugh at his tasteless joke, but the children didn't even react. Rose stiffened slightly but said nothing. The girl was small and slight, and possibly pregnant too – she had a neat little bump. She was around seventeen years old, the same age as me, with shoulder-length brown hair like mine, and she was eating a red ice lolly. There was no way this middle-aged man could be her lover. Especially not when he had a wife, right here. I didn't like his joke much. I'd certainly never heard of anything like this before.

I gazed awkwardly at my shoes, until Fred said, 'Come on, girlies, I'll show you to your room.'

As he brushed against me, I caught a whiff of baked-in sweat and something rotten, like farmyard muck. It was a horrible smell, and I gagged a little. Deirdre and I hurried after him up to the first floor, where we were directed to a bedroom at the very back, overlooking the garden. The room was sparsely furnished, but it was perfectly adequate. There was a double bed, a sink, a table with a kettle on it and a wooden chair. And by the bed was a small chest, two drawers high.

'I'll find a cot,' Fred said, and he was off again.

He seemed to have a slight limp, though I wasn't sure if that was just the uneven way he walked. He seemed an ungainly sort of man, in every sense. Looking around the room, I spotted what looked like six black circles in the wall adjoining the landing.

'Dee,' I whispered, peering more closely. 'Are they holes? Spyholes?'

We had to straighten quickly and smile as Fred returned with a cot. This time, he seemed to be limping half-heartedly on the other leg. The moment he left, we looked again at the holes.

'They look deliberate,' Deirdre said. 'Made with a screwdriver probably. Ew, how creepy. Do you think he's a dirty old man, with a lover and a wife, and he spies on his lodgers while they're getting undressed?'

'No.' I laughed and flung myself onto the bed. 'That was just a joke. No way that girl is his lover. She's only the same age as me!'

As we unpacked, Deirdre discovered she had forgotten one of the baby's bags, including his spare bottle. It was only a short walk home, so we nipped back to collect it.

'We've got a room at the Wests,' I told Mam, while Deirdre went upstairs. 'Cheap as well.'

'Oh, that's good.' Mam seemed relieved. 'Fred West is a good sort, I've heard.'

I felt rather pleased with myself as we made our way back to Cromwell Street. We'd landed on our feet. The Wests' living-room door was closed when we went in, but the hallway glowed with an eerie red light from the glass above the door of a room at the end.

'Maybe they're planning a disco,' I joked, as we parked the pram and made our way upstairs.

Back in our room, the holes in the wall were making me a little uncomfortable. I stripped off my blue T-shirt to rinse through in the sink, ready to wear again tomorrow. But I felt self-conscious in my underwear, as though I was being watched. Hanging my T-shirt on the back of the chair to dry, I spotted some yellowing sheets of newspaper on the floor, where the carpet didn't meet the wall.

'There,' I said, scrunching the paper into balls and blocking the holes. 'He won't see a thing now, whoever he is.'

With the baby settled, Deirdre and I had an early night too.

'These pillows are flat as pancakes,' I complained, folding a jumper underneath to plump mine up a bit.

Lying under a heavy brown cover and a green bedspread, I reminded myself how lucky we were to have found this place – cheap, clean and friendly. But a gnawing feeling of unease nibbled at my brain. As I drifted off to sleep, the anxiety ate away at me. And yet there was nothing at all for me to worry about. In the morning, I was first awake. Rolling over, I spotted six small balls of newspaper on the floor.

'Dee,' I gasped, shaking her awake. 'Look!'

The night before, it had seemed like a bit of a joke. But this was proof that someone was spying on us. Worse, he – or she – didn't seem to care that we knew it.

'What do we do?' I said, jumping out of bed and pushing them back into the holes.

'What can we do?' Deirdre shrugged. 'We've just paid a week's rent. We've no money, nowhere else to go. We'll just have to put up with it. You never know, it might be one of the kids just having a laugh, trying to scare us.'

I nodded uncomfortably, knowing she was wrong, and knowing she knew it too. For the rest of the morning, I threw myself into cleaning, my old cure-all. The room wasn't especially dusty, but I needed to clear my mind. I sacrificed an old T-shirt and washed the windows and then scrubbed the table. Further down the landing, I found a brush and swept the carpet the best I could.

'We've got the cleanest bedsit in the whole of Gloucester,' Deirdre joked. 'Trust you, Kathy.'

Later, we walked to Linbar's, the local supermarket, and shopped for packet soups, baby milk, biscuits and crackers.

Though we hadn't much money between us, we enjoyed being in charge of our own finances and choosing our own food. Neither of us had any intention of cooking, despite there being a cooker for the lodgers' use on our landing. On our way home, I spotted a corner of carpet hanging out of a skip in the street, next to a shop that was being renovated.

'No,' Deirdre said firmly, reading my thoughts. 'No way, Kathy.'

But I was already climbing up the skip, tugging at the edges until I had a small roll under my arm.

'This is perfect for our room,' I said. 'We can carpet the area by the door and use those newspapers to keep filling in the holes!'

For some reason, we both found that marvellously funny, and we laughed all the way home. Because that's what it was now: 25 Cromwell Street was our new home.

10

The next day, I was back at work at the factory on an early shift. On my way home at lunchtime, I bumped into the teenage girl, Shirley, carrying her shopping.

'Here, let me help you,' I said, taking a couple of bags. 'I'm Kathy Ryan.'

'Shirley Robinson,' she replied.

'You shouldn't be carrying this heavy shopping,' I told her, looking at her stomach. I wasn't sure if she was pregnant or not. But she handed me a couple of bags with a shy smile.

'Thanks,' she said.

I smiled back. 'If you need help any time, just shout. I'm in the end room on the first floor with my sister and her baby.'

We'd reached the front door by now, and Shirley stopped and rested her hands on her back while I found my key.

'I didn't believe Fred West's joke about you being his lover,' I said, feeling I should address his claim. 'He shouldn't have said that. It wasn't funny. I know he's not your boyfriend.'

I was trying to reassure her, but she replied: 'Course he is. I'm pregnant, too, due next summer. The baby's his.'

'It is not!' I laughed. 'Do you play this joke on all the new lodgers?'

Shirley pursed her lips, and a shadow passed over her face. 'You believe what you want,' she said flatly. 'The baby is Fred's.'

I searched her face for a flicker of humour but there was nothing. She seemed, if anything, a little sad. More than that, she looked lost and unsure, a small boat cut adrift on the waves. At the top of the staircase, I put the shopping bags down and tried to change the subject.

'Which one's your room?' I asked, pointing at the doors down the landing. 'I'll carry these bags in for you.'

Shirley shifted from one foot to the other, but didn't reply at first. 'Just leave them here,' she said eventually. 'I can manage. I'm fine.'

She wasn't unfriendly exactly. But I got the feeling she was hiding something and didn't want to confide in me.

Back in the bedroom, I said to Deirdre: 'Do you remember Shirley, that girl from yesterday? She just told me Fred West is her boyfriend after all. And she's definitely pregnant and wait for it – he's the baby's father. What do you make of that?'

Deirdre wrinkled her face up in disgust. 'No way!' she giggled. 'Imagine getting into bed with an old man like him and touching his Thing and having to kiss him!'

We shuddered in unison.

'He smells,' I whispered. 'He smells so awful. No way she could stand for that. She must be joking.'

In the afternoon, Deirdre was busy trying to settle the baby. She had just laid him in the cot when the most awful racket started under our window. We both recognised the familiar whining of a drill and, looking out, we saw Fred standing in the garden engrossed in some sort of DIY project. The Wests' garden was long and narrow, with paving slabs at one end, and grass at the far side. Fred was digging a hole there, his spade stuck in the earth while he drilled into a plank of wood on the ground.

'It's just like being back home,' I sighed. 'Fred's like Dad, don't you think? Always renovating something. I wonder what he's making.'

Deirdre nodded towards the hole. 'Maybe he's digging a swimming pool!' she joked. 'We might need our bikinis when the weather warms up.'

As we giggled, Fred suddenly looked up at our window with a comically exaggerated wave.

'He thinks he's so funny,' I said, thinking again of Shirley and the riddle of her pregnancy. 'Look, he's limping on the other leg today. It was the left side yesterday.'

As he walked down the garden in the fading light, his bad leg swapped back to the left again. He lifted his arm with another wave and I couldn't help laughing. There was definitely something a little odd about Fred, but he seemed harmless enough, like a real-life clown.

A couple of days later, I bumped into Shirley again, sitting on the wall outside, with an ice lolly in her hand.

'I'm off to Linbar's,' I said. 'Do you want me to get you anything?'

She slid down off the wall. 'I'll walk with you,' she said. 'I'm feeling peckish.'

I was wary of bringing up the subject of the baby again and

instead we chatted idly, complaining about the cold weather and comparing our favourite Top 40 songs.

'I love the Bay City Rollers,' I told her.

Shirley was pretty quiet until she heard I worked at Wall's, and then her eyes widened with envy.

'I've had such a craving for red ice lollies since I got pregnant,' she said. 'Working there would be my perfect job!'

When we came out of the supermarket, Shirley handed me a paper bag with a pasty inside.

'My treat,' she said.

'Thanks,' I grinned.

She'd bought a sausage roll for herself and, back at the house, I followed her into the main kitchen, which belonged to the Wests.

'Are we allowed in here?' I asked anxiously.

Shirley gave a half-smile. 'Oh yeah,' she replied. 'Don't worry about that.'

The kitchen was a long, narrow room at the back of the house. Right in the middle was a pole, floor to ceiling, which I recognised as a by-product of a DIY disaster. I thought back to Dad moving the entire bathroom suite downstairs and I smiled. He and Fred were so similar, and it made me feel at home here. Shirley switched on the electric grill and slid the pasty and the sausage roll underneath. As we waited for them to warm through, Rose appeared at the kitchen door. She didn't speak but, walking past Shirley, made sure to nudge her firmly with her shoulder. The silence that followed, broken only by the humming of the grill, was tight with tension. After Rose's back was turned, Shirley raised an eyebrow at me.

'What was that about?' I whispered, as soon as Rose was gone.

But Shirley just raised the other eyebrow and said nothing. I was beginning to understand that Rose was not a woman to be messed with. If Fred was afflicted with too much humour, then Rose had none at all.

Despite the noise, the smells and the peepholes, we settled in well in those first weeks at Cromwell Street. The room was a little bigger than we were used to, and I enjoyed the freedom and space. All my life, I'd been jostling for position with other bodies, squabbling over a scrap of food or a corner of blanket or a spot by the fire. Here, I could do almost exactly as I liked. I loved stretching out in the double bed. But, according to Deirdre, I still took up far too much room.

'You're like a starfish,' she'd say when I woke each morning. 'Honestly, Kathy, I was hanging onto the edge of the bed all bloody night. I've not had a wink of sleep.'

The room had no radiator, or heating of any kind, and it was freezing cold, especially in the mornings. Deirdre wore a fake fur coat she'd found in a charity shop and often buttoned it over the baby on her chest. I wrapped myself in the rough green blanket from the bed. But somehow, being cold became a fun activity. We enjoyed huddling up together and marvelling at the steam clouds every time we breathed.

'Cheaper than smoking,' I joked.

We found increasingly inventive ways to block the holes in our bedroom, too. After we'd used all the newspaper up, we collected a bag of twigs in the park and bent them into shape to fill the holes. But the next morning, the twigs were scattered across the floor like broken fingers.

'Who on earth is doing this?' I asked.

Next, as Deirdre pushed the pram through the park, I searched for pebbles to slot into the holes.

'What do you think?' I asked her. 'Too big?'

We laughed in mutual horror as we weighed each one up for size, arguing over whether it would be too big or too small. But the next day, as always, the pebbles had been pushed out onto the floor and the holes were clear.

'I can't believe I didn't even hear the pebbles falling onto the carpet,' I said. 'Tonight I'm going to stay awake. I've had enough. I'm not letting them see me naked, whoever they are!'

Deirdre and I both laughed. It was becoming a battle of wills. After those early feelings of unease, we had almost started to accept the peepholes as part of everyday life. We were light hearted and happy-go-lucky, in the way that teenagers are. Nothing bothered us too much; all distress was temporary. Besides, deep down, we didn't really believe there was a sinister motive behind the peepholes. There were so many children in the house, people coming and going, and it was impossible to work out who lived there and who didn't. The peepholes were, we decided, the work of a practical joker. I made myself a strong coffee and vowed to stay awake to catch the culprit.

'Well, I'm not missing my sleep,' said Deirdre. 'I'm up early with the baby.'

By 3 a.m., the pebbles were still in place, and my eyelids drooped heavier and heavier. Maybe, I told myself, the peeping Tom had learned his lesson. Maybe we'd scared him off. Towards 4 a.m., I must have nodded off. In the morning, when I opened my eyes, I was stunned to see the pebbles in a line on the carpet.

'I don't believe it!' I shrieked. 'I'll never catch him!'

Angrily, I pushed the pebbles back into place. Deirdre and I went out all day and when we got home in the evening, the pebbles were on the carpet again. Even while the room was empty, the mystery spy had been busy at work. This was, I realised, as much about control as it was about spying. Whoever it was wanted us to know they, not us, were in charge.

'I'm not giving up,' I said. 'I'll keep filling the holes.'

'And he'll keep emptying them,' Deirdre said. 'I doubt we'll ever find out who's behind it.'

I had to admit, she was probably right.

11

The routine in the West household was that there was no routine as such. Fred, though he was a handyman and DIY fanatic, did not have regular work. Yet he was always on the go, always in the middle of some project or other. We'd often hear him drilling or hammering in the cellar or see him digging in the back garden. Neither Deirdre nor I had ever been in the cellar. It was accessed by a small door, no taller than 5 feet high, and kept permanently locked. But Fred was down there much of the time and the hammering and drilling in the depths of the house reverberated right through the floors.

'He's at it again,' we'd say, rolling our eyes.

Or we'd spot him digging outdoors, with his black jacket hung over the fence as he flung soil through the air.

'Finishing off that outdoor swimming pool,' we smirked.

Cromwell Street itself was noisy, too, and most, if not all the houses, had been converted into bedsits, mainly occupied by students from the college nearby. Some of the more rundown properties had an old chair or a mattress in the front garden. The odd one had a boarded-up window. But most of the houses were well kept, probably thanks to Fred's handyman work. The street was blocked off at the bottom end, which led to a car park belonging to Linbar's. The top end was near to the gates of Gloucester Park. There was a small corner shop on the street, a church and also a milk delivery depot. At night, the red and white milk floats would all be parked outside, ready for the early-morning deliveries. Most of the neighbours were nice and friendly and would say hello as we passed. And as darkness fell, mixed in with Fred's banging and clattering were sounds of shouting, screaming, laughter, arguments and fights. It was, in every way, a normal street in a normal town.

Number 25 had many rooms over four floors, including the cellar, and it was sometimes difficult to work out whether the noise came from our building or one nearby. On some mornings, the incongruous sound of a choir from the church next door would float in through the windows, adding to the potpourri of sounds.

Quite often, one of the landlords on the street would knock on the Wests' door, to ask if Fred could fix a leaking pipe or un-block a toilet. Nothing seemed to be too much trouble for him. I witnessed him abandoning his dinner one day to rush out and help with a plumbing crisis. I even saw him ushering students into his car, to give them lifts into the city centre or beyond. There he was, making his silly jokes, limping on the wrong leg and grinning inanely. He seemed a little eccentric, a little irri-tating, but good-hearted all the same. The whole neighbourhood seemed to rely on Fred for handyman work.

One day, as Deirdre and I were carrying the pram out of the

front door, Fred popped up and said: 'Can I offer you girlies a lift somewhere? No trouble.'

'No, thank you,' said Deirdre politely. 'We'll walk. The baby needs some fresh air.'

He stood and watched us, grinning ridiculously, as we walked off down the street.

'He's an oddball,' Deirdre said, when we were out of earshot.

'He means well, though,' I replied. 'Or at least I think he does.'

Rose didn't have a job, either. She seemed to spend a lot of her time in the Wests' living room or in her bedroom. The Wests had the whole of the ground floor, along with some rooms on the upper floors. The lodgers were housed on the first floor, which had a separate bathroom and a cooker. Including ours, there were three rented rooms on the first floor and I presumed there were three more upstairs, though I never ventured up there. Another lodger, a young woman, told me Fred was planning to build a separate kitchen for the rented rooms, but I was quite happy to live on biscuits and cup-a-soup. Part of the thrill of leaving home was avoiding household tasks like cooking. The only thing I really missed was my regular cleaning routine.

Week by week, I saw so many unfamiliar faces coming and going from the house that I struggled to keep track of who lived there. The Wests had lots of visitors, mainly men on their own, especially in the evenings. I couldn't work out who was visiting and who was renting. Often there was a strong smell of cannabis coming from the lodgers' rooms, which made me wary of starting a conversation with anyone. And so apart from chatting with Shirley, who I was growing to like, I kept myself to myself.

Certainly there was no obvious work ethic. Nobody seemed to

leave for work in the mornings or come home in the evenings. Soon it felt like I was the only one on the whole street with a regular job and, aged seventeen, my motivation for those early starts and long hours on the production line quickly drained away. Mam was not here to make sure I was out of bed early each day, and I overslept several days in a row. I began to see the world of work as an unnecessary chore. Eventually, seduced by the promise of an easy life, I handed in my notice at work and instead signed on the dole. Mam must have heard I'd left my job, and she knocked on the door of Cromwell Street that same week, her lips pursed with disapproval.

'Why have you given up work?' she demanded. 'You need another job, Kathleen. You have to learn to support yourself.'

But I no longer needed to listen to her. For the first time ever, I had nothing to do, nowhere to be and nobody to boss me around. It was at once exhilarating and unsettling. I did not understand why, but there was a temporary, fragile feeling to my days, as though this state of affairs could not possibly last.

Deirdre had many friends, including a boyfriend, in Derby and she often went back to visit overnight, taking her baby with her. When my sister wasn't around, I'd spend my time with Shirley. We were becoming good pals, bonding over our love of ice lollies and our daily trips to Linbar's, and I was pleased to have found a friend. But though I did not see it at the time, our connection ran much deeper than that. Part of me felt sorry for Shirley, not realising that she probably felt sorry for me, too. Lost and untethered, we grasped at each other as though our heads were sinking below water, not knowing whether we would pull each other down further or keep each other afloat. Looking back now, it's clear we could not have saved ourselves, let alone each other. But at seventeen, anything seemed possible. Shirley's problems seemed to mirror my own and in her, subconsciously, I saw a lot of myself – a young and frightened girl, running from her past and desperately trying to live for her present. Superficially, though, she and I were quite different. I was an average young woman in many ways, surrounded by the ephemera of the typical teenager. I bought *Jackie* magazine whenever I could afford it, and I taped posters of Bay City Rollers and Showaddywaddy onto the bedroom walls. Though I didn't own many clothes, I had my blue T-shirt, which I washed every night to wear again, paired with my beloved flared jeans and denim jacket. It was fashion on a shoestring, but it was fashion all the same. Shirley, on the other hand, seemed old and frumpy beyond her years. She had bypassed teenage culture completely and showed little interest in music, fashion or make-up. She wore two or three shapeless dresses with floral designs, which accommodated her pregnancy but were more suitable for someone three times her age. She wore her brown hair loose; I never saw her with a ponytail or even a hair slide. She didn't seem to give her appearance much thought. I wondered if she was ageing so quickly because she was dating an older man, yet each time I looked at Fred, and that smell hit my nostrils, I questioned whether that story could really be true.

One day, I walked to the market and treated myself to a long row of cheap silver bangles, which reached right up to my elbow. They were the height of fashion – everyone had them, and I loved the way they chimed together as I walked. I ran into Shirley on my way back into the house and her gaze immediately settled on my new bangles.

'Here,' I said, slipping off a dozen or so. 'I've plenty, you can have these.'

She hesitated. 'I don't know if Fred will like them,' she mumbled.

'Well, they're not for Fred, they're for you,' I replied, completely missing her point.

'No, no,' she explained. 'I mean Fred might not like me wearing them. He might not allow it.'

I stared at her in astonishment. 'That's ridiculous,' I replied. 'It's none of his business. If you like them, you take them.'

Shirley accepted the bangles with a grateful smile and looped them over her wrist. Her arms were even skinnier than mine. I could tell she loved the bangles, yet I never saw her wear them again. And despite our developing friendship, Shirley still stuck to her story that Fred was the father of her baby. As the weeks passed, I was a little hurt that she didn't confide more in me. She rarely made any reference at all to her baby, except to say, 'Fred and I will raise it together.'

One afternoon, as we walked to the shops, I plucked up the courage to tell her exactly what I thought: 'He's an old man! I don't know how you do it. Have you touched his Thing? Do you sleep in the same bed?'

Shirley shrugged vaguely without replying and I realised, as I spoke, that I didn't even know where her room was. She always seemed to hover awkwardly on the landing, like a fading apparition, until I'd closed my own door. And the next time I looked out, she'd be gone. Though we were pals, she was as mysterious and out of bounds as the cellar, which was kept locked at all times. And the more I pressed her for information, the tighter she clammed up, a tiny creature inside a shell, retreating from the world outside.

We had been at Cromwell Street less than a month when Fred instructed us to pay our weekly rent directly to Rose.

'Don't give it to me,' he said, with an exaggerated shudder, as though he dreaded the consequences.

When, later, I found Rose in her living room and handed over the money, she took it without a smile or a thank you. She did not even look straight at me, instead giving me a haughty sideways glance from under her eyelids, as though she could not be bothered to look properly. I got the distinct impression I did not merit her time or her effort.

'That Rose,' I fumed, when I got back into the bedroom. 'Honestly, she's so stuck up.'

'Did she look at you sideways?' Deirdre asked. 'She does that to me, too. I hate that, it's so rude. She's weird.'

From then, we paid our rent directly to Rose and, if it was ever late, she'd send Fred upstairs, like an obedient dog, to remind us. In the mornings, we'd hear her yelling at the children, or possibly at Fred. Or maybe even at someone else. She'd scream and swear, her harsh voice bouncing off the walls around the house. And sometimes we heard the children screaming, too. Yet we were used to that; the mood in our own house was noisy and confrontational and our father was prone to outbursts of violence. So we barely gave Rose's temper a second thought. Besides, it was none of our business; we would never have dared question her behaviour.

One chilly afternoon, Deirdre and I were lifting the pram in over the front step, and Rose screeched, 'Shut the pissing door!'

'That Rose,' I muttered, when we were out of earshot. 'She's so grumpy. How are we supposed to get the pram in without opening the door?'

Another time, at around 7 p.m., we came home from a long evening walk to settle the baby. We made barely any noise but as we pushed the pram through the hallway, Rose yelled: 'Be quiet! I have visitors here!'

Deirdre and I rolled our eyes. A parent herself, Rose seemed to have little patience and even less empathy with other mothers. She made as much noise as she liked, right through the day and night, and nobody ever mentioned that. Her demands were unfair, but we were used to that, too. Face to face, we were painfully polite and deferential towards her, but in the privacy of our room, she became 'that Rose'. Deirdre and I did impressions of her contemptuous sideways glances, laughing out loud at each other's efforts.

'Mine's the best,' I insisted.

'No mine is,' Deirdre argued.

Yet there was another side to Rose. On one occasion, Deirdre had already taken the baby upstairs and I was struggling to collapse the pram in the hallway. An affected voice behind me, which sounded like it belonged to a five-year-old girl, said, 'Oh dear, it looks like you're having trouble there.'

I was stunned when I turned around to see Rose. The voice sounded nothing like her, the manner even less.

'I can manage, thank you,' I mumbled.

Rose used the same syrupy tone when Mam called round one day to check on us.

'Girls,' she said sweetly, without a trace of her usual Gloucestershire accent. 'I do believe there is someone at the door for you. I do believe it's your mother.'

Deirdre and I exchanged glances. The giggles bubbled in my throat, but I would not have dared laugh at her.

'Thank you so much,' I replied, in the same formal manner.

Another day, I saw Rose leaving the house wearing white ankle socks and a short black skirt. She looked as though she'd borrowed a school uniform from one of her daughters.

'Oh, I've seen her wearing those white socks, too,' Deirdre confirmed, when I saw her later. 'She dresses like a child sometimes. Very strange.'

It was as though Rose had several distinct personalities. One was rough and ready, screaming, swearing and yelling abuse in her heavy West Country accent. Another self was the complete antithesis – softly spoken and prissy, with a silly, simpering tone. She had a third persona too – she could be boisterous and forceful when she was drunk. One evening, she flung open her living-room door and invited me in.

'Come and join the party!' she shrieked. 'Come and meet Mandy!'

The room was already busy with visitors and Rose smelled strongly of booze. I had no idea who Mandy was, but I didn't want to meet her.

'No thank you,' I stuttered. 'I don't drink.'

I scurried upstairs quickly to the safety of the bedroom where Deirdre was waiting.

'Oh, that Rose is a weird one,' we both agreed.

Luckily, we rarely needed to go downstairs unless we were leaving the house. Our cooking efforts stretched only as far as soup in a cup, which we made using our own kettle. But one day, I spotted a block of cheese on offer in Linbar's, and I bought it, along with a loaf.

'Cheese on toast!' I said to Deirdre.

We couldn't work out the grill on the upstairs cooker. I wasn't sure it was even plugged in. And so we crept downstairs to use the cooker in the main kitchen. We had never been told it was out of bounds – there were no rules as such in the West household. Yet it felt somehow risky, all the same. As I was watching the cheese bubble and brown, Rose appeared in the doorway, stony-faced. She stood, legs apart, arms folded, eyes wide yet strangely vacant.

'I'm j-j-j-just using the grill,' I stuttered, my hands trembling. 'I w-w-w-won't be long.'

Rose blinked slowly, like a lizard, and said: 'You make sure you clean that up.'

In itself, it was an innocuous command. But each word was loaded with hostility. My skin pricked as I slid the toast onto a plate and ran the hot tap. Rose levelled her gaze as I rinsed the tiny flecks of cheese from the grill pan. And though her eyes were completely without expression, I felt them drilling through the back of my head. The aggression emanated from her like heat. Normally, I'd have been itching to grab a cloth and give the whole kitchen a good scrub. I really missed cleaning sinks and cookers and fridges. But I had to get out of there. My appetite suddenly gone, I replaced the grill and picked up the plate of toast.

'Thank you,' I muttered.

I had presumed, when we moved in, that Fred was in charge of the house. He was loud and blustery and certainly the clown and the frontman of the family. Yet I was beginning to appreciate that, skulking in the background, Rose had a vice-like grip on the way things were done. While Fred was giggly and silly, she was malevolent and iron-willed. She was not a woman to be crossed, and I made a silent vow never to borrow her grill pan again. But all of this made Fred's claims about being Shirley's lover so much more outlandish. There was no way Rose would stand for such humiliation and accept her husband's pregnant girlfriend, living under her own roof. It was absurd. Rose didn't even let us open the front door without losing her temper. She'd never let Fred have an affair right under her nose.

Rose watched me scurry from the kitchen, balancing my toast, before following behind. I heard the bunch of keys on a string around her neck, swaying and clinking. Presumably they included the cellar key, too, the perfect metaphor for her position. She was, without doubt, in charge of Fred and the whole house. I was beginning to understand that. I remembered my mother choosing the name for her tenth child, and my father's unexpected acquiescence. Marriages, I realised, were difficult to assess from the outside. Things were never quite as they seemed.

12

I had been at the West house for around six weeks when I bumped into Fred in the hallway one morning. It was not especially long or narrow, but was cluttered with a couple of bikes belonging to the other lodgers, and often there were wooden planks or boxes of tools stacked against the wall, depending on what project Fred was working on. On this particular morning, he was carrying his usual assortment of tools, including a garden spade. I stood to the side as he approached.

'This is tight, isn't it, girlie?' said Fred with a wink, even though there was plenty of space.

But as he passed, he squeezed right up against me, his foul breath wafting directly into my face. Shrinking back from the smell, I suddenly tensed as he reached around with his free hand and squeezed my bottom.

'Lovely arse, girlie,' he smirked, and then he was gone.

Stunned, I almost wondered whether I'd imagined or misread the movement. Yet he had made the comment. It had to have been deliberate. My heart sank, wondering whether Fred was going to turn out the same as the caretaker and my grandad. It seemed to me that no man was to be trusted. But, an expert in denial, I told myself it was only a minor slip, and I decided to ignore it and hope it was a one-off. Besides, what else could I do?

But the very next day, Fred cornered me again, this time outside my bedroom.

'Give us a kiss,' he leered, thrusting his face close to mine.

He had a wide, doughy face, as though there was too much flesh squashed into a small area. His eyes, black as coal, were alight with mischief. I stepped back, more alarmed at first by the stench of dead animals than by his demands.

'Play the game,' he wheedled. 'Come on. I'll show you a surprise.' He patted his crotch, leaving me in no doubt as to what his surprise was.

Small and agile, I managed to duck under his arm and run down the stairs. I heard him laughing manically as I dashed out of the front door, up the path and onto the street to safety.

'Fred tried it on with me today,' I told Deirdre. 'I hope he's not going to be a pest.'

But from then on, Fred seemed to take every chance he could to seek me out and grope me. He appeared as if by magic in the hallway every time I went out, slapping me on the behind or pushing himself up against me.

'You know you want to see what's in my pants,' he smirked, grabbing himself through his trousers. 'You'll love him, girlie, I know you will.'

I was wary of annoying Fred – he was our landlord, after all. Yet the prospect of seeing his Thing repulsed me. I batted away flashbacks of the caretaker's hut and my grandad's living room.

For years, I had buried these memories so effectively, yet I was plagued by them now, so vivid that I relived the horror all over again: those bottle-green trousers, the sweaty, rubbery feel of the Thing, the reward of the coin in my small hand. I could not go through all that with Fred. Yet I didn't have an escape strategy, either.

But Fred seemed different to the others, too. He was full of smiles and energy. He saw the funny side of everything. Each time he tried to grope me, I managed to wriggle away. He didn't try to stop me or even complain, rather he'd usually burst into laughter and make a silly comment.

'I'll get you next time, girlie!' he'd shout, as though it was all a hilarious game.

Maybe, I told myself, I was being dramatic. I had no idea of what was acceptable. Perhaps I needed to lighten up a little. But one day, when I was alone in the bedroom, Fred tapped on the open door, wearing his usual stupid grin. I had no chance to react as he walked in, pushed me backwards, onto the bed, and shouted, 'You know you want it!'

'No!' I protested. 'No! Please leave me alone.'

He rolled me around on the bed, giggling as though it was an innocent wrestling match. Yet his hands were all over me.

'Stop!' I pleaded.

I managed to scrabble away, out onto the landing, down the stairs and into the street in my bare feet. I had left Fred in the bedroom but there was no way I could go back up there to lock the door and secure our room. Eventually, Deirdre came home and we went inside together, but there was no sign of Fred.

'You're going to have a keep an eye on him,' Deirdre warned.

In the days afterwards, I did my best to avoid him, but it

wasn't long before he ambushed me again, trapping me in the bedroom on my own and again pushing me onto the bed.

'My sister's coming!' I yelled, knowing she was miles away in Derby. 'She'll be back in a minute!'

I wriggled and fought against him, but Fred had my arms and legs pinned down. He stank of sour sweat and muck and his breath was every bit as revolting as his body odour. I could not help worrying, even in that moment, that my bed would smell of him, and I resolved to wash the sheets as soon as it was over. But as his hands pulled at my clothes, I began to panic.

Over the hammering of my heart against my ribs, I heard a voice shout, 'Leave her alone, Fred!'

It was enough to startle Fred, and I took my chance to roll out from under him. Shirley stood at the door, her face impassive.

'Are you OK?' she asked calmly.

She seemed neither shocked nor angry, nor even mildly surprised.

'I was only playing with you,' Fred said reproachfully, as though I'd made a fuss over nothing. 'It's a game, girlie.'

I felt a little guilty. If Fred thought I'd overreacted, perhaps he was right? He was the adult, after all. And everyone liked him. He was far more popular than me. So maybe I was the problem, not him. Even so, I didn't relish bumping into him again. The next day, we needed supplies from Linbar's and, as quietly as I could, carrying my shoes in my hand, I crept downstairs. As I got to the bottom, I saw the living-room door opening and I spotted Fred's mop of woolly hair from the back. Sucking my breath in, flattened against the wall, I inched back up the stairs. He was hopefully going out. The click of the front-door latch would mean I was free. Instead, I heard his footsteps on the stairs. He was coming after me. On the top step, I hesitated.

'Well, hello.' Fred beamed, showing me his crooked teeth. 'What are you up to?'

I tried to reply, but my mouth wouldn't even open. My mind was blank. Fred put one arm around my waist and his other hand on my shoulder. He pulled me towards him, lips parted, his tongue protruding slightly.

Suddenly, in panic, I found my voice. 'Get off me!' I shouted. 'Go away!'

But Fred began rubbing his face on mine, like a bizarre mating ritual of a wild animal.

'You will love the games we play,' he giggled, scratching my cheeks with his sideburns.

In the background, mercifully, I heard the sound of people chatting, and two young men came past.

'Let me go!' I yelled, and it was enough for Fred to step back. He sauntered off across the landing, limping slightly, as though nothing had happened.

Another morning, again needing supplies, I went out to Linbar's to buy milk, bread and a packet of digestive biscuits. I managed to get out of the house without a problem. But on my way back in, with my arms full of shopping, I dropped the biscuits on the landing as I fumbled for the door handle. As I bent to pick them up, I felt a sharp slap on the bottom and a mocking voice said, 'What a great arse you have!'

I shot up, leaving the biscuits on the floor, coming face to face with Fred. I banged on the bedroom door, hollering Deirdre's name and, when it opened, I fell inside.

'You don't need to bang like that!' she huffed.

In whispers, I explained what had happened. But even through the closed door, we could hear Fred giggling like a deviant child. Though I didn't believe he meant me any real harm, I was unnerved at the way he seemed to materialise from out of the walls and the carpets. Wherever I went, he seemed to be hiding, ready to pounce.

'Let him cool off for a few days,' Deirdre suggested. 'He might get bored and give up.'

I took her advice and remained in the bedroom with the door locked as much as possible.

But one morning, someone shouted: 'Kathy Ryan! Your mother is at the door!'

I had no choice but to go down. Mam had been calling round each week to check on us. I always enjoyed seeing her, and often she had a couple of my younger siblings with her. I hadn't been back home since we'd left because I was keen to avoid my father and his temper, and so this was my only chance to catch up with them all.

'How are you?' Mam asked, with her bag looped over her arm. 'I'm going shopping. Do you want to come?'

Cagily, I shook my head. I wanted to go to the shops, but I didn't want to risk meeting Fred on my way back.

'I'm fine,' I mumbled. 'Thanks.'

We said our goodbyes and, as I turned back into the house, there was Fred, a laughing ogre, a twisted clown. I was trapped, as helpless as an insect with a pin right through me. In one respect, the hallway was the perfect lair for him; I had no escape. I would not have dared to run through the doors leading to the Wests' living areas, even though it was often busy with strangers arriving and leaving. That did not seem to bother Fred at all.

'I want to show you what I've got in here,' he said, thrusting his crotch at me. 'You're going to like him.'

'Shirley!' I yelled at the top of my voice, desperately hoping she was at home.

To my relief, she appeared on the stairs. She did not even need to speak; Fred backed away as though she was operating him by remote control. And though I was shaken, I had to admit I was fascinated by the hold she seemed to have over him.

'Come on, I'll make you a brew, let you get your breath back,' she offered. 'Honestly, he's nothing to worry about.'

But I was so cold at my core, shaking and trembling, and no amount of hot tea could soothe me. I found myself choking back tears as Shirley patted my hand. She wasn't a tactile person, and this was her version of a hug.

'It's not just today,' I said tearfully. 'He's done it before. He won't leave me alone. And have you seen the spyholes in our bedroom wall? I think someone is watching me.'

'I think you're probably right,' Shirley replied. 'But honestly you shouldn't get upset. It's no big deal.'

And I tried to tell myself that, too. The peepholes were no big deal. Fred's behaviour was no big deal. And in the 1970s, social and sexual attitudes towards women certainly were very different to now. Back then, he fell into the category of 'dirty old man' with 'wandering hands'. There was almost a benevolence in the language, a passivity, an acceptance that it was just the way some men were. Everyone knew someone like Fred – a wayward relative or an oddball creepy neighbour. I did not think for a moment that it was worth a complaint, or that anyone would believe me. Fred was a middle-aged man and I was a child. He was a husband, a father and a well-respected figure around the neighbourhood. Compared to him, who was I? My self-esteem, already eroded by the abuse in Dublin, was almost at the point of implosion. But Fred's behaviour made me question again the source of the peepholes. Was he the culprit after all? Shirley had seemed to think so. And could it be that she had been telling the truth all along about her baby? Perhaps this was how he'd started off with her, grasping and groping and playing the fool, before getting her pregnant. My blood curdled at the idea he might have similar plans for me. Yet Fred's persona as a harmless buffoon made it impossible to be truly afraid of him. Even his limp, and the way it migrated from one leg to the other, was a reflection of his personality, an indication that he was not to be taken seriously. He did not seem in any way sinister or scary. In his own words, the whole thing was just one big game to him. If this was a false identity that he had cultivated in order to target young girls, then he was an excellent actor.

And overlaying all of this, like the heaviest of weights, was my own history. In my mind, Fred's behaviour linked, quite naturally, with the attacks by the caretaker and by my grandad. The abuse seeped, like a leaky pipe, into every area of my life, and I accepted it as my fate, as something that happened to girls like me. All men were the same and Fred simply proved the theory. Since the age of eight, I'd been abused time after time after time, and what was more, I deserved it. Fred would never have targeted a nice girl like Sally from Derby, with her rows of lovely dolls, or Diane, the teacher with the fairy-tale wedding. They were nice girls, from nice homes, and they met only nice men. But I was fair game. I was the perfect target. I was damaged goods.

13

Christmas 1977 came around and though we'd never celebrated Christmas living at home, I was looking forward to
sharing a bottle of lemonade in the room with Deirdre. I didn't
like drinking alcohol; my only vice was a cigarette, when I could
afford it. On Christmas Eve, Deirdre and I were pouring out
our lemonade when Fred knocked at our door.

'Rose is out for the night,' he said. 'Who fancies coming down
to play some party games with me and the kids?'

I looked at Deirdre, silently willing her to refuse. She stared
back, evidently hoping for the same from me. After a few uncomfortable moments, I muttered: 'My sister needs to settle the
baby. We'll be down soon.'

'Well, don't be long,' Fred replied.

Deirdre and I sat glumly on the bed after the door had closed.

'How are we going to get out of that?' I said under my breath.

In whispers, we came up with a plan to pretend we'd gone out.
I volunteered to creep downstairs and slam the front door hard,

before tiptoeing back up again. Then we switched off the light, got into bed and finished our drinks in the dark. It was much more fun than it sounds, huddled up under the scratchy green blanket, trying to breathe quietly while collapsing into helpless giggles. We had such a lovely Christmas Eve and the thought that we'd outwitted Fred made us happier than ever.

Christmas Day was unexpectedly quiet, considering we were in a house full of children. It struck me as peculiar that the West house, chaotic and noisy on every other day, was by contrast deserted on the most family-orientated day of the year. There was no Christmas tree, no gifts that I could see and the only nod to the festive season was a scraggy string of tinsel slung around the bottom of the banister. This household seemed to work in opposition to the rest of the world. Back then, I did not dwell on the differences. After all, my own family did not celebrate Christmas, either. There were many similarities between the Ryans and the Wests – or so I thought. Deirdre and I shared a family bag of cheese and onion crisps for breakfast on Christmas Day as a nod to the festivities, before going for a walk in the local park. When we returned, the house was still silent. There were no party games and no smell of roasting turkey. No whooping children or tipsy parents. It seemed like any other day. In fact, the place was eerily empty.

Soon after the new year, I turned eighteen, and Deirdre took me to the Pop-In cafe in Gloucester, our favourite venue for treats, to celebrate with a fried breakfast.

'You're officially a grown-up,' she beamed, as we clinked our mugs of tea. 'Congratulations, Kathy, you're getting old.'

But truth was, I'd felt ancient and world-weary ever since that first time I'd stepped inside the caretaker's office.

*

I was on my way out one brisk March morning when I bumped into Fred and Rose on their way in. Though I disliked Rose, I felt safe from Fred's advances with her there. Rose was wearing a scarf and a thick black coat.

'It's really rather cold outside,' she said to me, using her silly, formal voice. 'And it's forecast rain. You'll need a coat, Kathy.'

I was pleasantly surprised; she had never seemed concerned for my welfare before. And she was right, too – I was wearing my favourite blue T-shirt and denim jacket and already I could feel a cold draught through the open front door. But I didn't own a coat.

'Thanks, but I'll be OK,' I replied.

Rose walked past me into her living room, but Fred held the door open. I tried to scurry quickly past him, but he said: 'Hang on, you can take my jacket, girlie. We can't have you going out in this weather in a thin jacket, can we now?'

He took off the jacket and draped it solicitously around my shoulders. Then he put both of his arms around me and clasped me so tightly it took my breath away. I stood there, rigid and terrified, my arms pinned by my sides. It was horrible, yet I felt shouting out might be an overreaction. I was aware Rose was just a few feet away, too, and I was worried about causing a fuss. Fred pressed himself right up against me, laughing as he squashed his face into mine, rubbing his bristly chin and side-burns into my eyes and mouth. All the while, he squeezed me harder and harder, until I thought I was going to burst.

'Stop!' I gasped. 'Stop! It's too much!'

Fred was still laughing when one of his daughters, with the same mop of black hair as him, came out of the living room and stared at us both.

'Meet your new friend, Kathy,' Fred said, grinning.

The girl said nothing. I felt sick and dizzy as he squeezed again, so hard that my feet left the floor and I heaved violently. Then, without warning, he dropped me like a rag doll, picked up his jacket, which had fallen to the floor, and walked away. Stumbling outside, I made it to the pavement before I vomited. Disorientated and nauseous, I tried to ignore the sharp pain across my temples. But as I made my way back upstairs to my room, I felt the walls crowding towards me and bright lights flashing painfully at the back of my eyes. I had just made it through the bedroom door when I suffered a seizure. When Deirdre came home, I was lying on the bed, on top of the covers.

'What's happened?' she asked. 'You look so pale, Kathy.'

'I had a seizure, Dee,' I said weakly. 'Fred grabbed me and squeezed me. It was awful. I know he thinks it's a game, but I don't like it.'

The tears streamed down my cheeks as she took my hands in hers.

'You're safe now,' she soothed. 'Don't worry.'

Though I hated them, these attacks from Fred simply became part of my life. Just like the abuse from the caretaker and my grandad, they were something to be endured with as little fuss as possible. While they were happening, I felt like I was being swallowed whole and devoured piece by piece by a rabid monster. Like a river about to burst its banks, the emotion churned and swelled within me. Yet just four or maybe five hours later, I snapped back to my old self. Subconsciously, I developed an ability to disconnect and to brush each episode of abuse from my mind, as surely as if it had been painted over with a fresh new colour. I managed to convince myself that the most awful aberrations were in fact minor blips. And always lurking, at the root of every thought, was the belief that it was all my fault anyway.

Alongside Fred's advances, my days were peppered with the sound of Rose screaming and him hammering and drilling. This noise became the soundtrack to my life at Cromwell Street. Yet I was happy there, too. I enjoyed the freedom and the independence. I looked forward each day to spending time with Shirley – our leisurely strolls to the supermarket or simply swinging our legs on the wall outside. At those times, Fred seemed like nothing more than an annoying pest. Shirley would have been the most obvious confidante for me but, somehow, I could never bring myself to tell her about each new attack. Instinctively, I sensed she did not want to hear the details and I was worried about pushing her too far. She was like a tortoise, cautiously poking her head out into the sunlight, but always ready to pull back and hide. Besides, she already knew what Fred was like. She had rescued me from his clutches more than once. And I didn't understand why she wasn't jealous or angry. If he was her boyfriend, why would she allow him to make advances towards me? Why would Rose allow it? There was something I was missing. None of this made sense.

'They're a funny lot here,' I said to Deirdre one night, as we were getting into bed. 'Rose screams the place down if one of the kids leaves a door open. Yet she doesn't seem to mind her husband trying it on with the lodgers. She doesn't even care that Shirley claims to be having his baby! I can't work them out.'

'Me neither,' Deirdre agreed.

We didn't understand why Fred didn't target Deirdre, either. Possibly, it was because she was away in Derby sometimes. Maybe, we reasoned, it was because she had a baby. Only with hindsight now do I understand that it was Deirdre's character that probably saved her. She was straight-talking and she took no nonsense. Knowing she could look after herself made me feel that I was all the more blameworthy because I couldn't, that the abuse was my fault. But from day to day, as teenagers, we didn't look at things that deeply.

'Maybe he just doesn't fancy me!' Deirdre giggled. 'Perhaps he likes your jeans and jacket, Kathy. Maybe he's got a fetish for denim!'

We both shrieked in disgust at the thought. Even the suggestion of a man like Fred having any kind of sexual urge was grotesque. We thought that people of his age didn't even have sex. He seemed so old to us. Such insouciance was both the best and the worst aspect of being eighteen years old. I didn't worry much at all – not even when I really should have.

One morning, Shirley and I went on one of our shopping trips and I insisted on carrying all the bags. By now it was April, and she was heavily pregnant, maybe seven months, though she was characteristically vague about her due date. She still refused to discuss the baby at all. I had no idea whether she wanted a boy or a girl, where she planned to live or how she was going to manage. All she ever said, as if reading from a pre-agreed script, was, 'Fred and I will raise it together.' I had given up prodding her for more details. For whatever reason, she didn't want to tell me the truth.

Back at the house, I headed for the stairs with the shopping. But Shirley pushed open the Wests' living-room door and beckoned me over. Walking through the doorway, still carrying the bags, I suddenly stopped dead in my tracks. My legs threatened to buckle, as though the strength had been zapped out of me.

'Oh,' I whimpered, the tiniest, involuntary sound.

The room was dimly lit with a standard lamp in the corner. It was empty except for Rose, who was reclining on the sofa, her legs wide apart, her eyes typically blank. Her face was plastered with garish make-up – blood-red lipstick, bright eyeshadow and a heavy foundation. She had no shoes on and was wearing a short, completely see-through nightdress and nothing else. An embarrassed blush crawled up my neck and across my face. I didn't know where to look. This was the first female body I had ever seen and, as I squeezed my eyes closed, I hoped it might be the last. It took me a few more moments to process that a squelching, groaning noise was coming from the television. When I dared to turn my head and open my eyes, I caught sight of naked bodies writhing around on a table.

'Come on,' Shirley said, inclining her head towards me.

But I was rooted to the spot, as surely as if I'd been nailed down in one of Fred's DIY blunders. Rose did not speak and I could not bring myself to look at her again, though I knew I'd never be able to erase her naked image from my mind.

'See you later, Shirley,' I mumbled, backing rapidly out of the room.

I fell into Deirdre, who was on her way in, and I steered her back towards the front door.

'I have to get out of here,' I whispered. 'Quick.'

Once we were outside, hurrying down the street, I told her about Rose, posing naked on her sofa, and the pornographic video she was watching.

'Oh, that Rose is disgusting!' Deirdre exclaimed. 'And what was Shirley thinking, taking you in there?'

As she spoke, I realised I was still carrying Shirley's shopping.

With a sickening thud, I also realised that she hadn't followed me out of the living room. We walked back to the house but I couldn't find Shirley upstairs. I left her shopping on the landing and, a little while afterwards, I spotted her and Rose going into the Wests' bedroom downstairs. With instant and painful clarity, the penny dropped. I realised now why I had never seen Shirley going into her own bedroom. She didn't have one. She shared with Fred. And, seemingly, with Rose. I felt sick with confusion. At eighteen, I'd led a relatively sheltered life and had never had a serious boyfriend. But this was a level of depravity that any adult would have struggled to comprehend. Frustrated at my own naivety, I realised Rose had been trying to seduce me, competing, quite incredibly, with her own husband. It was mind blowing. I kept insisting to myself that I'd misunderstood, that there was another more rational explanation. But why else would Rose have lured me into the living room? And though I couldn't admit it to myself, I knew, deep down, that poor Shirley must have been coerced into this, too. She'd been forced to set me up, invite me into the living room and hope I'd agree to whatever Rose had in mind. I was being groomed. But who by? Fred? Rose? Or both?

14

That strange incident with Rose, running parallel to Fred's behaviour, made me even more nervous. I got into the habit of running down the stairs and through the hallway as fast as I could, as though the place was on fire. It was like dodging landmines. Many times, I had to endure the ignominy of Fred bursting out and slapping my bottom or grabbing a breast before I made it to the safety of the front door.

'Nearly there, Kathy,' I whispered, as my fingers curled around the door handle.

The fresh air on the other side had never smelled so pure. But while I dreaded being intercepted by Fred, I also saw it in the context of a teenager who took nothing very seriously. If I made it out of the house without seeing Fred or Rose, I'd allow myself a celebratory giggle. Aside from those mad darts through the house, I did not let them worry me too much. That said, I was keen to avoid Rose, maybe even more so than Fred. That repugnant image of her in her lingerie was one I knew I would carry with me for ever. And though Fred and Rose seemed to pop up like boils every day, their children were curiously absent. On that first day, when Deirdre and I had arrived, the living room had been bursting at the seams with little ones. Now, I never saw them. But it wasn't my place to question that.

One night, when Deirdre was away in Derby, I had a nice long bath. I was busy drying my hair afterwards when the hairdryer suddenly cut out and the lights went off. Creeping onto the landing, I saw there were lights downstairs, so the problem was obviously limited to my room. In my dressing gown, I tapped tentatively on the Wests' living-room door.

'Come in,' came Rose's voice, and I could just imagine her haughty sideways glance as she spoke.

I opened the door, and it was like a savage flashback to my last visit here, except there was no dirty film on the television. Rose was on the sofa, again in her see-through nightie, again leaving absolutely nothing to the imagination. The sight brought me out in a cold sweat and my stutter got the better of me.

'Th-th-th-the electric's g-g-g-gone,' I whimpered.

'I'll send Fred,' she replied calmly, with her usual look. Her eyelids were so heavy that they looked hooded and vulture-like. The thought of Rose as a bird of prey, in her chiffon slip, made me want to retch. The bile hit the back of my throat as I bolted back upstairs. Realising I could not find my clothes in the darkness, I waited on the landing.

'Let's get this sorted,' said Fred cheerfully as he appeared beside me, carrying his toolbox.

I followed him into the bedroom as he flicked the light switches a couple of times.

'So,' he said, shining a torch as he rummaged in the toolbox, 'you off out to meet your boyfriend tonight, then?'

I shivered involuntarily. Without replying, I began towel drying my hair vigorously and, with the light of the torch, I managed to grab my denim jacket, T-shirt and jeans from the back of the chair. My plan was to get changed in the bathroom and then leave the house until the electrics were fixed.

'Well' – I cleared my throat – 'I'll leave you to sort that out, thank y—'

But before I made it to the door, Fred pushed it closed with a soft click.

'Aah, no you don't,' he said, and even in the gloom, I could picture his stupid grin. He flicked the switch again and the lights came back on, illuminating his doughy face, his rotten teeth and his deranged smile. He took a step towards me and my heart began to race.

'Deirdre will be home soon,' I babbled. 'She's changed her plans and she's due back any time now. She's bringing the baby, so I need to help her carry the pram in downstairs.'

Fred seemed to take this as an invitation, lunging at me with both hands around my waist and pulling me towards him. The smell, as he rubbed his face into mine, was putrid. He slid his hands onto my bottom and squeezed so hard that I screamed out in pain.

'Stop!' I begged. 'It hurts!'

Using my bottom as leverage, he lifted me off the ground until my shoulders were level with his.

Fred laughed. 'Play the game, girlie.'

'It's hurting!' I screamed. 'Please put me down!'

Suddenly, I was dropped to the floor, discarded like a piece of litter. Fred laughed as he walked out with his toolbox, leaving me in a crumpled heap. I managed to shut the door before I crawled, sobbing, into bed. Wobbly and queasy, I winced as my head began thumping with pain. I could feel a seizure coming, and I was enveloped in a darkness much thicker than the blackout of the earlier power cut. When I came around, moments, minutes, hours later – I had no idea how long – my bottom was stinging in discomfort. I couldn't bear even to lie on it and instead shifted onto my front. I stayed like that, almost catatonic, until Deirdre came home.

'Let me see,' she said, pulling back the bedspread.

I flinched in pain as her face creased with concern.

'It's really red and bruised, Kathy,' she said. 'He must have squeezed you so hard.'

For days, I could not sit down or lie on my back. I was in agony. Yet whenever I saw Fred, he was as jovial as ever. And surely, if his behaviour had been as abhorrent as I believed, he would behave differently. He would at least be contrite or sheepish. I found it so hard to work him out, and I questioned my own judgement. Perhaps I was the one in the wrong here. Yet whatever Fred was doing, it did not feel like a game to me.

My bruises were only just healed when, once again, Fred jumped out on me as I walked in through the front door. It was too late for me to turn around and go back out – the door had already closed – and instead I paused, unsure how to react. I was locked in a bizarre dilemma where I was expected to be polite to my landlord, while warding off his sexual assaults.

'Hello, girlie,' he said with his crooked smile.

'Hello,' I said anxiously.

There was a moment of silence, loaded with intent, and a shiver ran right down my spine and the backs of my legs. In the next instant, Fred had shoved me hard, into the wall, banging my head against the plaster. He held me there, in the hallway, his whole body pressed against me. I felt as though, in every sense, he was squeezing the life from me.

'You know you want me,' he rasped. 'You can't fool me, girlie. Rose isn't home. Why not come to my bedroom and see what I've got for you.'

When I didn't reply, he shoved into me that little bit harder and I cried out in pain.

'Get off me!' I screamed. 'Please just leave me alone!'

The Wests' living-room door opened and, to my surprise, Shirley emerged. By now, Fred had his elbow in my throat and I was gasping and choking. Yet he continued to smile. He either couldn't, or wouldn't, understand how frightened I was. Or perhaps that was all part of the thrill.

'Fred!' said Shirley sharply. 'Let her go!'

It was like a magic command. He stepped away and I slumped down the wall, sobbing. Shirley was walking towards me, asking if I was all right, but I was already on my way outside. I had to get away. I ran down the street, all the way through the park and onto the main road at the other side. When I stopped, breathless, sweating and doubled over, I was still crying. I was like an overloaded circuit: my tears were not simply from this attack, though that was horrific enough, but from everything that had gone before.

'It's not right,' I told myself, as I wiped my nose and eyes. 'I should report him.'

The police station was not far from the park and, filled with resolve, I made my way there. But by the time I arrived, I had stopped crying and my thoughts were more ordered. Reality settled on me like a heavy coat and, with a sigh, I slumped down onto the police-station steps. Who was I trying to kid? Fred and Rose were a lovely couple, well liked and well thought of, right through the community. Even their names sounded down to earth and friendly. *Fred and Rose.* They could belong to children's TV presenters, or a couple running a friendly seaside guesthouse. The police would never believe me against the Wests. They would never believe me against anyone. It was my place in life to be abused by men like Fred West, and it was time I got used to it.

There was also an element of self-interest in my decision, for much as I loathed what was happening to me, neither did I want to lose my home. I had nowhere else to go and, if I did leave, I might end up somewhere even worse. I walked slowly back to Cromwell Street, deflated and defeated, but resigned to my fate. It was late when I got back to the house, but Shirley was waiting up for me. As soon as I closed the door behind me, she came rushing out of the Wests' living room.

'I was worried about you,' she said. 'Are you OK? You mustn't take any notice of him.'

I hadn't known what to think of Shirley since that grotesque incident with Rose and her see-through nightie. I hadn't even been sure whether she was still my friend. So I felt such gratitude at her kindness.

'I'm OK,' I mumbled. 'More to the point, how are you?'

I nodded at her belly, which looked comically huge. The rest of Shirley was so skinny, it almost looked as though she had a balloon down her dress. If Rose was a vulture, Shirley was like a tiny sparrow, her arms and legs bird-thin.

'You must be due soon,' I added.

'Oh, I've a month or so to go yet,' she replied, characteristically vague.

She used the kettle in the Wests' kitchen to make us both a cup of tea, but she suggested we take it upstairs to my room. I got the feeling Shirley was increasingly uncomfortable being downstairs where the Wests lived. But I knew by now there was no point in pushing her for information. In the bedroom, she perched on the wooden chair and I sat on the floor.

'Look,' I said, pointing to a carrier bag in the corner. 'Deirdre's saving baby clothes for you, all the small ones she no longer needs. You don't need to worry about buying a thing, especially if it's a boy.'

Shirley managed a half-smile, but her eyes looked sad. She made me think of my little doll Polly, broken and lost. I had the feeling there was so much she was hiding from me and from everyone. She was like a paper fortune-teller, the game we'd played so often as children, folded in on herself, so many times. I would never get to the answers concealed at the centre.

She yawned. 'I should get to bed,' she said. 'I'm exhausted.'

When she left, I noticed she went into a room down the landing belonging to another lodger, a dark-haired girl I'd never spoken to. I caught sight of a sleeping bag on a sofa and realised Shirley must be sleeping there. In that moment, I was overwhelmed by a tidal wave of angst that prickled across my skin like electricity. Deep down, I felt something was terribly, tragically, wrong. But I could say no more than that.

15

May 1978 arrived and, with it, some sunny weather. This spring was not as hot as the previous one, which had preceded months of drought. But the weather was unseasonably warm, nonetheless. At night, we kicked off the scratchy green blanket and flung open the sash window to allow the cool air from the garden to drift inside. During the day, we wore shorts and T-shirts and positioned ourselves in the spots of sunshine that landed, like gold coins, on our carpet.

'This is a lovely time of year to have a baby,' said Deirdre, as she folded more baby clothes into the bag for Shirley. 'She must be due any day. It will be lovely for her, enjoying this nice weather and taking the baby out in the sunshine.'

I nodded and smiled. I hadn't seen Shirley for a few days, which was unusual. That evening, when the door was ajar, I peered into the room where I thought she was sleeping. But she wasn't there.

'Maybe she's gone to visit friends,' Deirdre suggested, but I shook my head doubtfully.

'She never really mentions anyone,' I said. 'She doesn't have any family nearby that I know of, or friends outside Cromwell Street. I can't think where she can be.'

The next day, still with no sign of Shirley, I was starting to worry a little. She was about to give birth, after all.

'What if she's in hospital?' I said to Deirdre. 'She might be in labour, right now. I need to find out, then I can visit.'

There was only one thing for it. I had to pluck up the courage to ask Fred myself.

'Who, Shirley?' he asked, his brow furrowed, as though he didn't know her too well. 'Shirley Robinson? Oh, she moved on.'

I stared, uncomprehending.

'Moved on?' I repeated. 'What do you mean? Where is she?'

Fred shrugged happily. 'No idea,' he replied. 'It was just time for her to move on. She's gone. That's the way of things, girlie.'

I was astonished. It didn't make sense at all. If he was her boyfriend and the father of her child, as he claimed, how did he not know or care where she was? Her one plan had always been to raise the baby with Fred. And why would someone so heavily pregnant just vanish overnight? She was only eighteen. I couldn't even check her room, because she didn't have one. I didn't know where she kept her belongings, or even if she had any. I had no idea who her family were or where they lived. There was nobody I could call or visit to check for news. I was beginning to realise that, though we were friends, I really didn't know much about Shirley. She had kept me at arm's length, a solid glass screen between us. But then, I had done the same with her, keeping my secrets locked away. But I'd never have left without letting her know. And, I couldn't deny it, I was a little hurt. Shirley and I were pals. Sure, she was a closed blind – private, guarded and shy – but I never dreamed she'd walk out without even saying goodbye. I was washed through with anger, fear, worry and confusion.

It was just time for her to move on.

But where? And why, and how? The questions bubbled around my head and I couldn't let them go. I went off to find Fred again, aware of the irony that I had spent months trying to avoid his advances, and here I was actively seeking him out. And now that I wanted to find Fred, he was suddenly unavailable. After weeks of him materialising in the hallway every time I left my room, he was nowhere to be seen. He was no longer ambushing me or groping me. It seemed he was busy elsewhere. For though we could not see him, Deirdre and I could hear the distant sounds of DIY. He was obviously in the cellar, banging, drilling and sawing. The noise kept us awake, it went on so late. Yet it was strangely comforting, lying in bed, listening to the sounds of Fred at work. It was a reminder of home, of our father's love of DIY, and it was a small comfort in the gloom as I mulled over Shirley's departure. I wondered about quizzing the other lodgers, but I didn't even know their names. Deirdre and I had always kept ourselves to ourselves, not even making eye contact with the others. I'd sometimes see a young man fixing his bicycle in the hallway, but we never got past pleasantries.

'Ey up,' he'd say, as he tinkered with his bike chain.

He seemed nice enough, but I knew he wouldn't be able to help me. As far as I knew, Shirley had never spoken to him.

'I'm going to talk to that Rose instead,' I decided. 'See if she knows where Shirley is.'

I could not bring myself to knock on the living-room door, for fear of catching Rose undressed again. Instead, I went down-stairs early the next morning, when I hoped she'd be making her breakfast in the kitchen.

'What happened with Shirley?' I asked, in a small, apologetic voice.

Rose glanced at me sideways from under heavy, reptilian lids. Before she'd even spoken, she'd made me feel I was wasting her time.

'She left,' she said abruptly.

'Do you know why?' I pressed, sounding braver than I felt. 'Or where's she gone? Or anywhere I could look for her?'

Rose shook her head grumpily and turned her back on me, and I had no option but to sidle quietly back upstairs. Pacing the bedroom, I fretted all day.

'There's no way she'd have just left,' I reasoned. 'No way. She didn't even take those baby clothes with her! Why would she leave those behind?'

I worked myself into such a panic that I began to feel sickly and light-headed.

'Dee, I'm going to have a seizure,' I gasped.

When I came round, Deirdre was holding my hand. 'You're OK,' she said gently. 'You blacked out, but you're back now.'

Deirdre didn't really know Shirley, but she offered to speak to Rose too.

'I'll do my best,' she promised.

She went downstairs but was back a couple of minutes later. Rose had dismissed her with the same sideways frown and the same short shrift that she'd given me.

The days passed, and I hoped there might be some word

from Shirley – a phone call or a letter. I even hoped she might come back. She'd have given birth by now, I realised. Perhaps she'd visit, to show off her new baby. I wondered whether she'd had a boy or a girl, and if she'd found somewhere to live. I just wanted to know she was OK. I longed for a postcard with a single sentence on it. But there was nothing at all. And, almost as bad as her being missing was that nobody seemed to notice she had gone. I had half expected that a midwife or a health visitor might knock on the door, looking for her. But, as far as I knew, nobody ever did. The police visited one afternoon, but only in connection with a neighbour's complaint about one of the lodgers smoking cannabis. That wasn't unusual – the other tenants were often in trouble for minor issues. There was never anything serious. Besides, I couldn't report Shirley officially missing because she'd left of her own accord. Her own landlord had confirmed that. Her disappearance was a riddle and, slowly, I came to accept that, for whatever reason, Shirley had upped and left without telling me. It was the only explanation.

'I wish she'd at least said goodbye,' I said sadly.

Alongside his project in the cellar, Fred threw himself into digging up the back garden again. Deirdre and I watched from the bedroom window as he flung great clods of earth over his shoulder.

'That's going to be some swimming pool,' I sighed miserably. 'I just wish Shirley would come back to see it.'

It upset me that our friendship had mattered so little to her and it was a further knock to my self-belief. My parents didn't want me. My own grandad had abused me. And now my friend had left me behind. Each night, for many weeks, I sobbed myself

117

quietly to sleep to the sounds of Fred clanging and banging in the bowels of the house.

'Where are you, Shirley?' I whispered.

But my only reply was silence.

16

Autumn came and Fred's attentions switched away from his DIY and back to me. My thoughts were again taken up with ways I could avoid him, though that didn't stop me fretting about Shirley, too. I remembered the way she'd helped and comforted me – even rescued me from Fred – and my heart ached. For the millionth time, I wondered why she had gone and where on earth she was. The bag of hand-me-down baby clothes waited forlornly in the corner of the room, as I hoped she might one day return.

One morning, as I was coming out of my room, Fred lunged at me and I raised both hands in front of my face in alarm.

But to my surprise he stood back and said: 'I've got some news about your friend. I thought you might like to know.'

'Shirley?' I gasped.

'Yeah, that's the one. Seems like the silly bitch went to Germany. She's living there now.'

'What?' I gulped. 'How far is that? How did she manage

that with no money? Who paid for the flight? And what about the baby?'

I was jabbering, but I couldn't help it. I had so many questions. But Fred ignored them all and was already limping unconvincingly down the stairs.

'Deirdre! I gasped, running back into the bedroom. 'Fred said Shirley's gone to live in Germany.'

'Germany is abroad,' she replied. 'No way she could get a flight. She was about to have a baby. I don't believe it.'

I racked my brains, trying to remember if Shirley had ever mentioned any relatives or friends in Germany, or any desire to visit. But she hadn't. I didn't know what to think. Deirdre was right, it seemed unfeasible that Shirley was in Germany, and yet I wanted to believe it. I needed to know she was safe and well somewhere. I was grateful Fred had gone out of his way to give me the update. He knew I'd been worried about her, and it was good of him to pass it on. Yet it was also very out of character. He hadn't seemed the slightest bit bothered when Shirley first vanished. He had been completely uninterested in my concern. So why now, all of a sudden, did he want to put my mind at ease? And though I desperately wanted the news to be a comfort, conversely it made me more and more concerned.

'I just don't think she's in Germany,' I told Deirdre. 'It doesn't make sense.'

'I know.'

'She couldn't even afford maternity clothes,' I said. 'How on earth would she pay for a plane ticket? And where would she find the money for a new home and a new life in a foreign country?'

Together, we stood at the bedroom window and looked out,

surveying Fred's latest DIY project. He'd finished banging in the cellar and he'd filled in the hole at the end of the garden. It was not a swimming pool after all. It looked like he'd just dug a big hole and then filled it in again, a completely pointless exercise. Now he was working on something that looked like a wooden shed.

'I wonder where Shirley is,' I said softly. 'I hope she's safe.'

As the nights drew in, Fred seemed to be at Cromwell Street all the time, and he focused his attentions firmly on me. On occasions, he jumped out, seemingly from thin air, like a panto-mime villain, making my heart race with alarm. I bumped into him so many times that it simply could not be coincidence. He appeared to spend his days loitering around the communal areas, waiting to strike. I had no idea whether he targeted the other lodgers too, though I doubted he'd have had the time. I could not fathom how, with his full-time job tormenting me, he also juggled his handyman work and looking after his many children. Not that Fred seemed especially involved as a father. Rose was the one who always seemed to be screaming and shouting at the children before the school run or at mealtimes, while Fred milled around the place with his silly smile and his temporary limp.

One day, I was hurtling down the stairs, thinking I had es-caped him, when I spotted him coming the other way. I stood aside to let him pass, wishing I could melt anonymously into the wallpaper. But Fred quickened his pace until he reached me, swapping his limp from one leg to the other, before it conven-iently vanished altogether. With his horrible grin, he pinned my arms by my sides and squeezed me hard.

'Now listen to me, girlie,' he said. 'If you come and play

some games with me and Rose, you and your sister can live here rent free.'

I was not so naive as to misunderstand his meaning.

'Well?' he cajoled, squeezing me a little harder, one hand crawling down my back and onto my bottom. 'How about it? No rent?'

My first priority was to get out of his vice-like grip. And, oddly, I was fretting about people overhearing him too. We were on the stairs and anyone could pass by and eavesdrop. I didn't want to get into trouble. No matter what he said about Rose, I didn't really believe she'd be pleased to hear him talking to me like this. And I felt she'd blame me and not him.

'Well?' pressed Fred as he groped my bottom.

'Yes,' I stammered. 'I'll ask my sister right now, thank you.'

Fred released me and I dashed back up the stairs and hammered on the bedroom door, even though I had my key. When Deirdre opened it, she was perplexed.

'I thought you were going out into town,' she said.

Quietly, knowing Fred was on the stairs waiting, I explained what he had said.

Deirdre whistled under her breath. 'Jesus. The dirty old pig. Is there nothing he won't do?'

'I know,' I breathed. 'He's disgusting.'

I had to cancel my trip out because I was too afraid of seeing Fred again, and instead Deirdre and I were holed up in the bedroom like fugitives. We didn't leave all day, except to nip to the loo.

'We'll go to the bathroom together, all three of us,' Deirdre said. 'I'm taking no chances.'

And so the room that had at first offered so much freedom

and fun now became a prison. The promise of liberation and in-dependence had been replaced by a stiff feeling of confinement. I was trapped, and I couldn't help fearing that this was exactly what Fred had in mind. Money was tight and between Deirdre and me we had very little left for luxuries. A rent reduction would have been wonderful. Yet no amount of cash could ever have persuaded me to join in with Fred's twisted little games.

When Deirdre was not away in Derby, she and I tried to stay as close to each other as possible, believing we were safer that way. Fred never bothered her and we hoped sticking together might persuade him to leave me alone too. One morning, she and I were planning to go into town together. But my favourite blue T-shirt was damp from the wash, and it was taking ages to dry with the hairdryer. Deirdre was in a hurry because she needed to get to the post office to collect her weekly benefits money.

'You go on ahead,' I said. 'I'll catch up with you at the post office as soon as my top is dry.'

It was a set of circumstances Fred could not possibly have known about. Yet ten minutes later, as I reached the bottom of the stairs all on my own, he dived on me with a gleeful grunt.

'Come here and see what I've got for you,' he said, his octopus arms reaching for my face, breasts and bottom, seemingly all at the same time.

'No!' I exclaimed, and I managed to get away from him and wriggle out of the door.

Another day, Deirdre and I were on our way out with her son when she realised she'd forgotten her bag. We carried the pram onto the path outside, and I said: 'You wait here. I'll nip back up for your bag. I won't be a minute.'

Taking the stairs two at a time, I sprinted up to the room, slotting my key into the door and leaving it ajar while I grabbed her bag, which was hanging over the wooden chair next to the bed. As I turned to leave, Fred's outline loomed in the doorway. He wore a fixed grin, as though it had been painted on. I froze. I didn't want to pass him, but neither did I want him to come any closer. It felt like hours as we both stood and stared at each other. I had to get downstairs – Deirdre and the baby were waiting for me. Taking a deep breath, I took a step towards the door, but Fred leapt into action as if this was what he had been waiting for.

As he reached for me, I shouted, 'Get out of my way!' much more loudly and bravely than I felt.

But Fred just laughed and threw me backwards onto the bed. He shoved his rough face into mine and it was as though he was slathering his own filthy smell all over my skin. He might as well have been spreading it across me with a butter knife. The stench was so intense, I could almost see it rising off him, like steam. It was as if he had rolled in muck; as though he had something dead and rotting hidden under his clothes.

'Stop!' I screamed. 'Help me!'

'Shut up, shut up, girlie,' he muttered as he rubbed himself against me.

In the next minute, I was aware someone was in the room. Fred sat back on his calves on the bed as Deirdre appeared at my side. Her face was white, her hands clasped tightly. She did not speak, but it was enough to put Fred off.

'I will have you,' he said, grinning as he walked out of the room past Deirdre.

Together, we clung to each other, neither of us able to speak.

'We need to go downstairs,' she whispered eventually. 'I've left the pram.'

As we walked up the street, I couldn't stop trembling. Digging my nails into my skin, I vowed I'd move out and find somewhere else – anywhere – to live.

'I can't take any more,' I whimpered. 'I really can't. We could ask Mam if we could go back home? She called round this week. She was asking how we were getting on.'

Deirdre sighed heavily and shook her head. 'They won't have us back, you know that.'

And by the end of our walk, I'd convinced myself, out of necessity, that it wasn't that serious after all. That Fred was just a clown, a joker, a dirty, dissolute old man who, at heart, was essentially harmless. This was the way with old men – the caretaker, my grandad and now Fred. His behaviour was following a well-worn path and just as I had run from the monsters once before, I reminded myself I could do it again. Fred was no danger to me and if I kept telling myself that, I might just believe it.

'OK,' I relented. 'We'll go back.'

But my heart was lead-heavy as I walked back through the hallway. I wondered, deep down, how long this could go on and how it would end.

Another day, I managed to evade Fred as I was leaving Cromwell Street, but instead he intercepted me outside as I was returning. It was early evening and I was walking down the street, coming from the direction of the park. It was raining heavily and, without a coat, I was dripping wet and cold to the bone. Through the rain, I could see Fred standing outside the front of his house, watching me as I approached, seemingly unbothered that he was getting soaked. My heart sank. I felt sure he was there for me, waiting to play one of his endless games. Yet I had no way of avoiding him. Even if I didn't go inside, I had to walk past the house. Besides, I needed to go in and get dry. As I reached the gate, Fred didn't stand aside to let me past and instead made a grab for me.

Lifting me off the ground, he sniggered. 'Do you want to come for a ride with me, girlie? Get out of the rain?'

Shocked that he would grope me openly in the street, my mouth opened and closed, but the words would not come. And then Rose poked her head round the side of the house. I expected her to be furious, or at the very least to object to Fred having hold of me, but she simply said, 'Oh, is Kathleen coming with us?'

'No,' I spluttered. 'No, I'm not.'

A couple walked past as I dangled there, and the man poked his head out from under their umbrella. Fred gave them a cheery wave, released me and I ran inside, choking back the tears. It felt like yet another narrow escape, yet another sliding-doors moment. What happened if, next time, those doors shut right in my face?

17

Deirdre was still making regular trips to Derby and one afternoon, late in 1978, I walked to the train station with her. Back at Cromwell Street, I did my usual dash along the hallway and up the stairs, relieved to find it was all clear. I unlocked the bedroom door and flicked on the light. A blade of fear sliced through me as I screamed at the top of my voice. For there, sitting on the bed, grinning idiotically, was Fred West.

'Hello, girlie,' he leered.

The blood pounded through my veins as I raced back down the stairs and out through the front door. I didn't stop running until I'd crossed the road and made it across the park. I had no idea where I was going, but I had to get away. For the next few hours, I walked aimlessly around the town centre, with no plan and nowhere else to turn. Finally, weak with hunger and exhaustion, I traipsed back to Cromwell Street. No matter how weary I was, how unsafe I felt, I had to keep coming back here. I had no choice. This time, I crept up the stairs, my heart thumping loudly in my ears. Cautiously, I opened the bedroom door, but he wasn't there. Nervously, I checked under the bed but the room was empty. Now, though, with the realisation that Fred had his own key and was happy to use it, I did not feel secure in my own room. Perhaps I had been naive not to suspect that before. Had he been snooping around in here while we were out? Worse, had he been snooping around while we were in? In panic, I remembered blacking out alone in my room when I had seizures. I had no idea what happened to me when I was out of it. What if Fred had let himself into the bedroom? What if he'd groped me, or worse, while I was unconscious? A cold sheen of sweat formed across my forehead as each possibility loomed into view.

'No, Kathy,' I told myself firmly. 'You're getting carried away. He's a pervert with wandering hands. That's all. He wouldn't attack you while you were unconscious. Calm down.'

But before I went to bed, I dragged the small chest of drawers across the doorway. They were not heavy enough to keep him out, but the sound of them scraping across the carpet would at least alert me if he tried to get in. And though it felt futile, I filled the peepholes with new pebbles from my walk. Lying in bed, too wired to sleep, I felt under siege, as if I was at war. I wasn't safe. Yet my enemy was a smiling, blundering buffoon, universally liked by the whole neighbourhood. My enemy was the same man who gave me a roof over my head. How could that be?

That same week, I went out to meet a couple of friends. I didn't tell them, or anyone else, about Fred West. Mostly, I tried to convince myself it was no big deal, and that I didn't need to confide in my friends. But, mostly, I felt ashamed. Just as with the abuse from my childhood, I somehow felt Fred's behaviour reflected badly on me. All the same, it was nice to see my friends and forget my worries for a while, and on my way home I treated myself to a bag of chips. I got them wrapped, because I knew there was a loaf in the bedroom and my mouth was watering at the prospect of a chip butty. I walked quickly so the chips didn't go cold. But as I arrived at the front door, I hesitated. I didn't want Fred to hear me arrive, and I slipped the key in as softly as I could, the door giving me away with a slight creak, before I tiptoed through the hallway. Breathing a sigh of relief, I put the key in my bedroom door. But as I turned the lock, someone grabbed me from behind. In shock, I dropped my chips on the carpet and they scattered everywhere. I was being held so tightly, I couldn't bend to pick them up.

'Help!' I yelled. 'Get off me! Help me!'

Even though he hadn't spoken, I knew it was Fred. That vile, feral stench gave him away. His odour hit the back of my throat and made my eyes water. It was so at odds with the wholesome smell of my supper.

'Help!' I shouted again.

But the house was eerily and unusually quiet, as though it was only me and him there.

'Come on,' said Fred with a throaty chuckle. 'You and me, let's have some fun. I'll show you what I'm made of.'

My throat ached with the threat of tears as I pleaded with him to leave me alone.

'My sister's back soon,' I sobbed. 'She'll be here in a minute.'

But Fred no doubt knew, as I did, that Deirdre was out. My key was still in the door and so, with one arm clutching me tightly, Fred used his other arm to open it. He shoved me inside and I landed on the carpet, shaking and crying. Then he closed the door behind him and pulled me up. Grabbing my face, he thrust his lips into mine, his bristly chin and sideburns scratching my skin. It was less of a kiss, more a show of aggression. I was horribly repulsed. To me, as a teenager, he was an old man. I didn't know whether the age gap or the smell upset me more. The issue of consent did not even occur to me. I didn't realise I was allowed to object to his assaults. I thought this was simply the downside of being me. Then there was the fact that he was married, and Rose would surely be angry if she found out. She might even evict Deirdre and me. And though, at times like this, I hated living here, I did not want to be homeless. The Wests were all we had.

'Come on,' Fred urged, pushing his face into mine more forcefully.

At eighteen, I was still naive, still unsure what relationships entailed. I'd never had a boyfriend. Yet I felt, in every aspect, that this was in no way normal. It was hard to breathe with his face clamped onto mine, and my breaths came in short, ragged gasps. Fred did not even seem to notice that I was sobbing and struggling. Looking back, I can see it was all part of the fun for him. He pushed me towards the bed with a grunt and, as my legs buckled, he landed heavily on top of me. He was stocky, I was small and slim, and I thought he was going to crush me. On one level, I was already crushed; a helpless ladybird squashed between finger and thumb. With one arm, he pinned my hands above my head and, with the other, he began grabbing at my body. I was wearing my usual flares and blue T-shirt and, to my horror, I felt his hands snake up inside my clothes and my bra. He had never gone this far before. I tried to call out, yet I couldn't make a sound because his mouth was on mine. I waited for him to move his head a little and then I took my chance to scream at the top of my voice. Fred had my arms, but I began kicking and booting him as hard as I could. I no longer cared about upsetting him or Rose or losing my home. This was about survival.

'Sssh,' Fred murmured. 'Just relax, girlie.'

The more I fought, the more aroused he became. He seemed to love watching me struggle. In desperation, I bit him on the neck, as hard as I could. But it didn't stop him even for a moment. He just turned his face to mine and sucked so hard at my mouth that it physically hurt. I feared my lips might actually detach. Panic coursed through me as he began tugging at the button on my jeans.

'Help!' I screeched, kicking out as hard as I could.

But Fred seemed immune to it all. As he was pulling my jeans down, a man's voice called his name outside my door.

'Fred?' he shouted. 'Fred? Are you in there?'

Instantly, Fred stopped. He clapped his hand over my mouth to silence me as there was a knock, and then another, on the door. I continued trying to kick and scrap, but Fred's hand was pressing so hard, I could barely breathe. A cold sweat was forming across my forehead, a metal taste filled my mouth and I thought I was going to have a seizure. Without warning, Fred stood up. Now, with nothing to restrict me, I was paradoxically paralysed with fear. Too afraid to shout out, or even to move.

'I haven't finished with you,' Fred said, and though he smiled, there was a malevolence in those words that turned my blood to ice.

With that, he marched out of the room, closing the door behind him. Slowly, I forced myself to move, robotically rinsing my face under the sink and then pushing the chest of drawers across the doorway. The details are hazy, but I think I suffered a seizure that day, alone in my bedroom. When I came round, it was morning, and I was cold and stiff, lying on top of the blankets on the bed. I had a pounding headache and a parched mouth, both of which usually followed a seizure. I have no idea who shouted Fred's name at the door – whether they knew what was happening to me, whether they even knew I was in that room. But they saved me, I am in no doubt about that. I owe them a lifetime of thanks.

Mam called round the day after Fred's attack. I was on the up-stairs landing when I heard a knock at the door:

'Could I have a word with Deirdre or Kathy please?' she asked.

The warm familiarity of her voice was like a gentle arm around my shoulders, and it brought me almost to tears. I hurried down the stairs to see her.

'Do want anything from Linbar's?' she asked. 'I'm picking up a few bits. We're out of washing-up liquid.'

'I'll come with you,' I said, so enthusiastic that I left without my jacket, even though it was a chilly day.

We walked in silence, Mam making the occasional comment on the weather or the traffic and me mumbling a response. On our way home, a vice-like pressure tightened across my chest as I tried to find the words to tell her what was happening to me. The tension was like a smog around me. I wanted so much to confide in her about Rose and Fred. About poor Shirley, too. More than anything, I was desperate to ask if she would have me back.

Can I come back home? I rehearsed silently.

Please could I come home? I'll get my job back, I'll do all the cleaning.

I'm frightened at Cromwell Street. I miss you all. Please, let me come home.

Mentally, I practised it over and over. Yet as we arrived back at Cromwell Street, I had said nothing. I hoped Mam might suggest it herself, that she might somehow intuit how miserable I was. But she and I had never shared that kind of connection. I knew I was kidding myself.

'So,' she said, as we reached number 25. 'See you soon. Behave yourself now. Tell Deirdre the same.'

And off she went, weighed down by her shopping and her own worries and oblivious to mine. The chasm between us, always there, felt wider than ever. That bond, that understanding, which I had longed for as a small child, had failed me then, and it failed me now. I knew, with all certainty, that I could not turn to my mother for help.

Only days afterwards, Mam called round again, this time to let us know she and Dad were moving back to Derby with the rest of the family, leaving us on our own in Gloucester.

'You be good girls,' she admonished, as though she feared we had already let her down.

The geography made little difference. I had been alone before, and I was alone now. Yet, after they had gone, I felt their loss keenly.

Christmas came around again, but I found it hard to get into the festive spirit. On Christmas Eve, I arranged to meet a friend to go Christmas shopping. She was going to pick me up on

Cromwell Street. I had only a few pennies, but I was hoping to pick up a toy for my little nephew in one of the charity shops. As I leaned on the gatepost, waiting for my friend to arrive, Fred came down the side path of the house and, standing behind me, made a grab for my right arm.

'Hey!' I protested.

But pinning my arm against my back, he began rubbing himself against me from behind.

'Come on in out of the cold,' he teased, nuzzling my neck. 'I'll warm you up. I will soon have you nice and toasty.'

My main concern, as an eighteen-year-old, was my friend's imminent arrival and her seeing Fred grope me. Mortified, I wriggled and tried to pull myself free with my left arm. But then Rose appeared at the other side.

'Come on, Kathy,' she wheedled in one of her silly voices. 'Come on inside.'

Rose seized my left arm, far too tightly, and panic pulsed through me. With her at one side and Fred at the other, I was immobilised.

'No!' I gasped. 'No! Leave me alone!'

A man walked past, just a few feet away, and I felt a flood of relief. I was sure they'd let me go. But Fred just laughed and shouted hello, waving with his free hand. Incredibly, though I was clearly in a tight clinch, the man just smiled and nodded in reply before carrying on along the street. He didn't suspect a thing. Fred was the local joker, the clown, the all-hours handyman. Why would anyone be suspicious of him?

'Come inside,' Fred urged again, his breath on my neck.

'Do as you're told, Kathy,' Rose hissed, her voice a sharp as a razor.

I screamed loudly, such a piercing noise that I shocked myself, and Fred took a step back and loosened his grip. Rose, too, stood aside and I pelted down to the far end of the street as quickly as I could. All thoughts of festive shopping forgotten, I didn't even dare go back to meet my friend. Instead, I wandered the streets, alone and upset, and when I got home late on Christmas Eve, Deirdre was worried.

'Where have you been?' she asked.

'Fred grabbed me outside the front door.' I shuddered. 'The weird thing was, Rose was there too. They were trying to drag me inside – they had one arm each. I don't know what they had in mind, but it really scared me.'

As I spoke, I felt a familiar hammer blow behind my eyes and there was a strong metallic taste in my mouth. With Deirdre's help, I stumbled onto the bed as a seizure took hold.

'You're all right, Kathy,' I heard her saying. 'You're back now. Just lie still.'

Christmas Day dawned but I didn't feel much like celebrating. Mam and Dad were settled in Derby and, apart from our brother, Danny, who had his own place, we had no family nearby. My parents were always on the move, always running, just like me. Most of my escapes were purely inside my head, and yet they were no less real. Did their physical movement link in some way to the running I did in my own mind? I wondered at the parallels and questioned why we were a family who could not, in any way, stay in one place.

18

Alone in the bedroom one January evening, I was engrossed in the latest edition of *Jackie* magazine. Deirdre had gone to Derby overnight to see her boyfriend; they wanted to spend more time together. When there was a light tap at the bedroom door, I answered it without hesitation. It wasn't Fred's style to knock on a door. I presumed it would be one of the other lodgers wanting to borrow a teabag or ask when the rent was due. So I was taken aback to see both Fred and Rose standing together in the hallway.

'What are you up to, girlie?' Fred asked, as Rose pushed past me and into my room.

It took a few panicky moments for me to find my voice. 'What's going on please?' I asked.

But even as I spoke, I chided myself. I had intended to sound angry and confrontational, but instead my voice was trembly and quiet. Fred laughed and grabbed my arm to pull me out of the doorway. Rose followed behind and, as Fred dragged me towards the stairs, my panic ballooned into all-out terror.

'Let me go!' I shrieked. 'Please let me go!'

But Fred was oblivious, frogmarching me down the stairs, so fast I thought I was going to trip and fall. I felt Rose's breath on my ear; she was right behind me.

'Stop!' I screamed.

Fred, still outwardly affable and smiling, clamped his free hand over my mouth and steered me into the Wests' family room. The curtains were drawn and the room was in darkness. Rose flicked the lamp on and shut the door. Fred's hand was warm and clammy on my mouth and the rancid smell, which seemed locked into his pores, hit the back of my throat and made me gag. He removed his hand and gave me a friendly smile.

'Relax!' he laughed. 'It's just a game, girlie. It's not like you were busy! We're just going to have a bit of fun.'

My heartbeat thudded in my ears like a fist thumping my head. I thought I was going to have a seizure. The threat of falling unconscious, with Fred and Rose standing over me, filled me with alarm.

'Stay awake,' I told myself fiercely. 'Stay awake.'

Rose sat on the sofa and patted the space next to her. I perched on the end, too afraid to disobey.

'You're overreacting, Kathy,' I said to myself. 'Rose is here. She won't just sit here and let her husband assault me. Maybe I'm safe. Maybe it's just a strange game after all.'

Rose sidled up to me and my blood curdled as she began stroking my hair. I felt as though I had a thousand ants crawling under my skin.

'Don't cry,' she simpered, in that silly, little-girl voice she used sometimes. 'Don't cry.'

Fred stood over me so that my face was level with his crotch.

'Have you got a girlfriend?' he asked. 'I know you don't have a boyfriend. Rose just wants to play with you, that's all.'

His rich West-Country accent sounded so unthreatening, completely at odds with the menace behind his words. Fear, dark and sticky like treacle, sluiced through me. I thought I was going to be sick. Fred stepped closer, rubbing his crotch against my cheek.

'Please,' I choked. 'Please stop.'

Rose took my face in her hand and turned my chin towards her. For a heart-stopping moment, I thought she was going to kiss me. Fred rubbed against me again and I felt his Thing hardening through his trousers. I tried to shrink back, to disappear down the back of the sofa into nothingness. Dizzy and disorientated, I questioned whether this was really happening, whether it was a nightmare, or maybe I was in the midst of a seizure. From hammering loudly, my heart felt like it had stopped completely. The silence in the room was suffocating. I could hear nothing at all.

And then the doorbell rang, shrill and insistent. The Wests had two doorbells, one for Rose and one for everyone else, and this was Rose's, the louder of the two. The sound was like a slap in the face, shocking me out of my stupor, and I jumped up from the sofa as though I'd been stung. Rose checked her watch, groaned angrily and stood up.

'Fred,' she rapped. 'Leave it. We're busy now.'

She went out to answer the front door and, as I ran past her, I heard her introducing herself as Mandy to someone on the doorstep. But I didn't stop to question it as I sprinted up the stairs and into the bedroom. My body knew it was now safe to have a seizure and, the moment I got through the door, I passed out.

When I came round, my face lying on my crumpled magazine, it was dark outside. I pulled the chest of drawers across the door and climbed into bed, sobbing.

How on earth was that a game? I asked myself. *How could that be normal?*

I drifted back to sleep, exhausted by the seizure. When I awoke the next morning, I had somehow downgraded the attack, in my mind, to a minor aberration. Fred and Rose were oddballs, I told myself. They had strange ideas about what was socially acceptable. But everyone else liked them. Nobody else had a problem with them. As the days passed, I implemented the same reliable technique I'd used as a child: disconnecting myself from the situation and denying there'd ever been a problem. It was all I knew.

In February 1979, Deirdre and I had planned to meet our aunt in Cheltenham for the day. But I woke with a dizzying headache and knew I was too unwell to go.

'I don't want to leave you here on your own,' Deirdre fretted. 'Not with Fred on the prowl.'

'I'll be fine,' I insisted. 'You go, she'll be waiting at the bus station for you.'

We had no way of letting our aunt know if we weren't coming. Besides, she had promised Deirdre some new clothes for the baby, which I knew were desperately needed. Deirdre was still unsure, but eventually I convinced her to go.

'I'll lock the door behind me. Make sure you pull the drawers across after I've gone,' she said.

But within moments of her departure, I was drifting off to sleep, the pain in my head mercifully easing a little as I dozed.

As I slept, I began to dream that there was someone in my bed, rolling me over, bandaging my lower legs in the blanket. Sweaty hands were slithering under my nightclothes, grabbing at me and groping my breasts. And then, suddenly, hideously, I was awake. With a rush of ice-cold terror, I realised this was no dream. Fred West was in my bed, pressed up against me. His dead-animal smell, like something decaying under his skin, escaped from under the blankets and smacked my mouth like a thunderclap. Yet the smell of fear was so much stronger.

'Please, no,' I whispered, so quietly I wasn't sure it was audible. 'Please, no. This can't be happening.'

I tried convincing myself I was having a nightmare. I wanted to wake up again and find myself alone and safe. Fred propped himself up on his elbow and leered down at me, his face looming over mine. He grinned insanely. He seemed unable to stop smiling, even when there was absolutely nothing to smile about. Was this how Shirley had got pregnant? Was this what he had done to her? Paralysed with fear, I squeezed my eyes shut and saw her face, pale, sad and scared.

'Please,' I begged. 'Let me go.'

But Fred only giggled.

'Now, girlie,' he said in a conversational tone, as though discussing his latest DIY plans. 'Me and Rose want you to watch a video with us. A special video, just us three. And then, girlie, we will have some fun. You get my meaning?'

His voice had a razor edge. And despite his infuriating grin, there was a warning in the way he tilted his chin. My whole body began to shake, so violently I worried I was going to have a seizure. My stomach churned, my throat constricted and I feared I might vomit out of pure fright. I remembered the pornographic video Rose had been watching in her living room the day Shirley and I had been out shopping. I knew exactly what Fred had in mind.

'Come on, girlie,' Fred urged. 'You'll love it, I know you will.'

I had no idea how to answer him. His hands were on me. His body was pressed against me. He had complete power over me. I had to be so careful with my response.

'OK, yes,' I replied shakily. 'I will. I'd like that.'

'Good girlie,' Fred smiled, squeezing me closer to him. He might as well have stapled us both together in one of his DIY projects. My mind was working furiously towards an escape strategy.

'I need the bathroom, quite urgently,' I said. 'Give me five minutes. I'll get changed into something. Something nicer.'

Fred's face lit up with joy. It was almost childlike, and my stomach frothed in protest.

'I'll go and tell Rose,' he said, swinging his legs over the bed. 'I'll see you downstairs in our living room. Five minutes, mind, no longer.'

'Promise,' I nodded.

The moment he was gone, I threw the blankets off me and leapt out of bed. Clutching at possibilities, no matter how out-landish, I ran to the window and looked out. But, as I already knew, it was far too high to jump from. I thought of hiding in one of the other rooms, but what if they were all locked? And what if Fred found me? I might not fob him off so easily a second time. My mind raced, but I couldn't think straight. I was running out of time.

'You can do it, Kathy,' I told myself firmly.

As quietly as I could, I inched my way across the room, out

onto the landing. I took the stairs slowly, stealthily, as though my life depended on it. And quite possibly, it did. I was afraid even to breathe, in case I made too much noise. My heart rattled so violently against my rib cage that I worried someone else might hear it. When I reached the hallway, I saw the door to the Wests' living room was closed. I had no idea if they were in there already. The tension was thick as I crept along the carpet. I felt I could have reached out and ripped a hole in it. It was like walking a tightrope, and falling off would mean certain disaster. Passing the living-room door, I heard the muffled sound of a television, and I breathed a silent prayer of thanks. At least the noise would drown out any telltale creaking floorboards. Though, of course the TV sound was confirmation they were definitely in that room. They were waiting for me. I reached the front door and there was a moment of heart-wrenching panic when the lock groaned slightly in betrayal, as though trying to alert Fred to my escape. But in the next minute, the cold outside air was on my face and I was running, running, running. Running from the monsters again. Like dominoes, the attacks formed a chain in my mind, until one fell into another and, one by one, everything collapsed around me. There was no going back. I knew that now. For over a year, my mind had simmered and boiled like a pressure cooker. But now, with a piercing screech, the lid was blown off. I did not even feel the pavement grit on my toes, or the wind whipping through my pyjamas. I was not even aware I was running barefoot, in my nightclothes, until I noticed people standing and staring. My pyjamas were hand-me-downs, and they were too big: I had to hold them up as I stumbled and floundered through the streets. I must have looked so strange, as though I'd escaped from prison. Which, in a way, I had.

'Are you all right, love?' called a middle-aged man in concern.

Dressed in overalls and a heavy coat, he was clearly on his way home from work; he was no threat to me. Yet I did not dare stop or even reply to him. In my eyes, every man was a risk. Half dressed, and with tears of mingled terror and relief streaming down my face, I continued to run. I did not stop once until I reached the bus station. I had no idea what time it was, or which bus Deirdre would be on. But I had to wait for her. I had no one else in the whole world. Curled up on the concrete floor of the bus station, in my blue pyjamas, I grew numb with cold and shock. It was spitting with rain, but I was thankfully under a shelter. Even so, I shivered as I rubbed my sore feet and waited. I learned there were two more buses due that day from Cheltenham. One was early evening, one much later. I hoped, with her little son in mind, Deirdre would be on the earlier one. It was already dark when the bus headlights, beacons of hope, swung around the corner into the station. Slowly, the passengers began to disembark, but there was no sign of my sister. My heart sank. Then the driver appeared, carrying a buggy I recognised. Forgetting my blisters, I ran to the bus doors in time to see Deirdre coming down the steps.

'Kathy!' she exclaimed. 'Why are you wearing pyjamas? What the hell's happened? Look at your poor feet, they're bleeding!'

I waited for her to stop talking and then it all tumbled out, my sentences like falling rocks, smashing the fabric of our lives apart. For I knew, for my own safety and sanity, there could be no more attacks.

'He was in my bed when I woke up, Dee,' I sobbed. 'I thought he was going to rape me. He wanted me to watch a video with him and Rose.'

'Oh God,' she gasped. 'Oh God. I knew I shouldn't have left you. I knew it.'

'I can't go back there,' I wept. 'I can't. That's it now, Dee.'

Deirdre put her arms around me, and we clung to each other in the rain and the cold, while bemused passengers made their way around us.

'Kathy, we need to go back for our things,' she said softly. 'We can't stay out all night, we have to think of the baby. I'm here now, I'll look after you, I promise.'

I didn't want to set foot in the place. I was adamant.

But Deirdre said: 'He won't do anything with us both there. I won't ever leave you with him again. Come on, you're safe now.'

Deirdre gave me her socks and her jacket to wear, and she led the way back to Cromwell Street. Like a small child, I trudged along behind her, with one hand holding my pyjamas up and my socks heavy and sodden as I splashed through puddles.

19

Arriving back, Deirdre turned her key confidently in the door and pushed it open.

'Come on,' she persuaded, taking my hand.

I knew it was an act, but she had always been more forthright and self-assured than me. There was no way she'd creep around the house in fear of Fred West, and it was no doubt that lack of fragility that had kept her safe from him. We got past the living room, up the stairs and into our room without seeing anyone. As Deirdre locked our door and blocked the way with the chest of drawers, I burst into tears of relief. I could hardly believe we'd made it. But then I looked at the crumpled blankets on the bed and again I could feel his rough hands on me and smell his rancid breath.

'I can't stay here,' I shivered. 'I can't.'

'We're leaving tomorrow,' Deirdre said. 'I promise you. We'll be gone before he wakes up.'

Peeling off my wet socks and pyjamas, I wrapped a towel around me and huddled on the wooden chair.

'Have a bath,' Deirdre suggested. 'It would warm you up.'

But there was no way I could risk leaving the room on my own. I could not bear to get into bed, either. For though I was icy-cold and bone-weary, there was no way I would ever lie under those blankets again. Deirdre handed me the green blanket and insisted I cover myself as I sat on the wooden chair.

'You'll never sleep,' she said.

'I know,' I replied, my teeth chattering. 'I don't want to sleep. I'll keep watch.'

Even though I was exhausted, adrenaline kept me wide awake. I had my eye on the door at all times, straining to listen for sounds on the landing. But there was nothing. By 5 a.m., I was on the point of collapse. Gently, I shook Deirdre awake and she got dressed. We had few belongings and it didn't take long for us to pack everything into carrier bags. It wasn't much to show for two lives. Still waiting forlornly in the corner was the bag of baby clothes intended for Shirley's baby. Deirdre had been adding to them every few months, as her own little boy grew.

'What shall we do with those?' I whispered.

'Might as well leave them,' Deirdre replied. 'We can't carry them. Though it's not as if she's ever likely to come back.'

But I quite liked the idea that the clothes would remain here, waiting for Shirley. It felt as though we hadn't completely given up on her, as though there was still a small glimmer of hope. One last time, I peered out of the window into the early-morning darkness, and asked myself where she was. No matter how much I wanted to, I just did not believe Fred's story about her new life in Germany.

'Shirley,' I mumbled. 'Where did you go?'

But my concern for her was soon eclipsed by more pressing

worries. Even as we packed, and checked under the bed and behind the drawers, we had no firm plan for the future. No idea where we might go.

Eventually, Deirdre said: 'Look, I can stay with my boyfriend in Derby. We've been talking about moving in together and so I know he'll be fine. And you could stay with Danny. He's much more likely to let you stay if I'm not there with a baby.'

I stared at my feet and tried to swallow back my tears. Even the suggestion that we were going to be separated pulled at my heartstrings. Deirdre and her little boy were all I had. But I knew she was right.

I nodded. 'Yes. Let's try that.'

As we crept down the stairs and through the hallway, I fancied I could hear the walls whispering to me through the hush of the dawn.

Run, Kathy, run. Get out while you can.

Even the door was quiet, the usual creak silenced, as though the house was doing all it could to help us on our way. It was still dark outside, and we carried the buggy out onto the path in silence. In the street, I turned to look at the house one last time. The windows stared back, black holes, like the peepholes.

Come on girlie, let me show you my boy . . .

As we made our final journey up Cromwell Street, Rose's voice rang out, shrill and harsh, in my head: *Shut that door! Keep the noise down!*

'I won't miss that Rose,' whispered Deirdre, as if reading my thoughts. 'Or Fred. They're a weird family.'

Our walk to the train station was surreal. My thoughts focused less on our departure from Cromwell Street and more on my impending separation from my sister. I had a lump in my throat all the way. As it grew light, Gloucester awoke and the hustle and bustle around us signified the start of just another day. Yet for us, it was a great step into the unknown, a leap off a cliff. As glad as I was to leave Cromwell Street, I was at once terrified of what lay ahead. And at that time, there was no sense of appreciation or relief. We had escaped – but we did not know what from. Only in years to come would our early-morning departure acquire heart-stopping significance.

Deirdre and I had one final hug on the station platform before I walked away, my heart sore and heavy. I had never felt so lonely. Tears sliding down my cheeks, I went into the station toilets to splash my face with cold water and get myself together.

'Come on, Kathy,' I said firmly, glaring at myself in the mirror. 'You have to stop this.'

Tapping at my brother's front door, I had a pre-prepared speech. The moment he showed me inside, I stumbled through it.

'I won't be any trouble at all, and I'm happy to sleep on the sofa,' I said in a rush. 'I've got my old job back at Wall's, so I'll be paying rent and bills.'

That last bit was not true, but I knew he would not accept me back if I was out of work. I was counting on my old supervisor taking pity on me.

'Well, I'm a bit short for the rent,' Danny replied. 'You can have the spare room.'

I could have flung my arms around him and wept with sheer relief. But that simply was not our way. Instead, I nodded gratefully and took my bag upstairs. I longed to get into bed and sleep, but I knew I had to get a job first. I was outside the factory gates before they even opened for the morning shift and recognised many of the old familiar faces as the crowd streamed through the doors. Luckily for me, there were jobs going, and the supervisor agreed to give me one last chance.

'No more,' he warned. 'Another day off and you're fired.'

I nodded gratefully. 'I won't let you down,' I promised. 'Things are different now.'

Again, I settled into a new routine, working long hours at the factory. Danny didn't live far from Cromwell Street and sometimes I'd find myself having to walk past the Wests' house. Their home was the epicentre of everything, magnetically pulling everything and everyone towards it. I could never truly escape the place. Yet I never dawdled on their street and I always walked on the opposite pavement. I was afraid of bumping into Fred or Rose. The memory of those long tentacle arms, dragging me towards them, sent a shiver down my spine. Once I spotted the back of Fred's tousled head and I darted behind a parked car, keeping my head down. He was chatting with a neighbour on the pavement and I heard him laughing and slapping his hand onto his jeans as he told another of his funny stories. How was it, I wondered again, that everyone liked him so much? Was I the only one who had a problem with him? And, if so, didn't that just prove that I was the one at fault, and not Fred?

Though I made plenty of friends at the factory, I never spoke to anyone about what had happened at Cromwell Street. I wouldn't have known where to start. In the first place, I wasn't convinced that anything of significance had actually taken place. There was still a gnawing doubt that I was oversensitive and overreacting. In my mind, I was already diluting and rationalising Fred's behaviour. Perhaps, as he said, it was all a bit of fun. And, for me, being abused and attacked, if not fun, was normal, after all. It never occurred to me that Fred might have been targeting others, too. As far as I knew, he had made advances only to Shirley and me, and Shirley was gone. But I think the main reason for my silence was an overriding, all-encompassing sense of shame. I was disgusted with myself. I felt grimy and unwashed. I could not seem to shift a layer of dirt that itched beneath my skin, acquired, as if by osmosis, from Fred. On bad days, I'd clean Danny's house from top to bottom, bleaching sinks, scrubbing skirting boards, polishing windows. The more I cleaned, the better I felt. And yet there was always one stubborn stain, one awkward spot that remained. And that was Fred West, and no amount of cathartic cleaning would ever remove it.

At these times, I missed Deirdre more than ever. Even when we chatted on the phone, or we got together for a visit, she and I never spoke of Cromwell Street. But it was enough just to have her near me, and to know that she understood. Without Deirdre around, I made more of an effort to see friends from work and soon I looked forward to Friday nights at the pub or Sunday afternoons at the cinema. One weekend, I got chatting to a young man called Davey who worked as a plasterer. He was the same age as me and incredibly good-looking, and kind and gentle, too. When he asked me out on a date, I felt my heart race with excitement.

'I've never had a serious boyfriend before,' I told him.

Within weeks, I had fallen madly in love. Davey's parents welcomed me into the family and, slowly, I began to believe that the happiness I'd always longed for might really be mine at last. Then, early in our relationship, I missed a period. Then another. I made an appointment with my doctor, and when a test confirmed I was pregnant, I was dumbfounded. Despite being sexually abused for most of my life, or perhaps because of it, I was incredibly naive. I had never even considered the possibility that I might fall pregnant. I hadn't even thought about birth control. In floods of tears, I rang my parents, hoping against hope they might offer me support.

'You're too young for a baby,' my father said. 'You'll never cope. You should get a termination. Do you hear me?'

'Yes,' I mumbled, tears blinding my vision.

I felt as though I was wading through a thick, green fog as I made my way to the train station. By the time I arrived in Derby, the arrangements had already been made. I had no other choice. People like me didn't get to make decisions. I knew and accepted that. I felt sedated even before I arrived at the hospital, as though my arms and legs belonged to someone else, as though my head was filled with cotton wool. My mind was completely blank until I lay down, on the hospital trolley, ready for surgery.

'I want this baby,' I whispered desperately. 'This is my baby.'

But a louder, more aggressive voice interrupted. *I do not deserve this baby. I do not deserve happiness. I am not good enough.*

That same night, I was on the bus back to Gloucester with a generic post-op leaflet in my hand. Staring out of the rain-streaked window, I was swamped by a regret so fierce that I could not breathe through it. But it was too late.

20

Those days and weeks following the termination were the very worst of my life. If I had felt lonely and desperate at Cromwell Street, then this was a level of despair I had never thought possible. Struggling under the burden of regret and remorse, I thought only of punishing myself. If I could have swapped my life for my baby's, then I would have done so in a heartbeat. With nowhere else to turn, I started attending Mass, as I had as a child. Sitting at the back of church, praying for forgiveness, I accepted there was no cure. My guilt was stamped right through me. But I found some comfort in the dusty pews and the familiarity of religion. Yet I felt something of a fraud, too. I didn't think I belonged in a church after what I had done.

Forgive me, Father, I pleaded, over and over.

I was convinced my baby would have been a boy, and that I would have named him Davey, after his father. I imagined him with the same blonde hair and bright blue eyes as his dad. When

Davey found out about the termination, he was understanding but insisted he would have supported me through a pregnancy.

'I had no choice,' I told him as the tears slid down my face.

It had never once occurred to me that Davey might stand by me. I did not feel I could expect or deserve that level of love or loyalty from anyone. His declaration just made me feel even more wretched. I loved him dearly but I knew our relationship was over. I could not bear to look in his eyes and see my lost baby staring back at me.

'I'm sorry,' I sobbed. 'I'm sorry.'

Davey wiped away my tears and promised he could forgive me. The problem was, I could not forgive myself. In the days afterwards, I sank deeper into depression. I lost my job, I stopped eating and I could not sleep. I rarely left my bedroom. My days began with a stinging stab of loneliness and self-loathing, and they ended the same way.

'You need to snap out of this, Kathy,' said Danny. 'You're making yourself ill. Why not come down the pub with me later?'

I shook my head miserably. Danny had no idea why I was so upset. I couldn't bear to confide in him about the termination. I was too ashamed. I didn't tell anyone, fearing they would judge me the way I judged myself. But, mentally, I marked a calendar with what should have been milestones – five, six, seven months into the pregnancy. I daydreamed constantly about the little boy I could and should have had. Each time I passed a baby in a pram, or I spotted a pregnant woman, I was overcome with grief. I missed Davey desperately, and I missed our baby, too. It perplexed me that I could miss someone I had never met. I felt my baby's loss so keenly that I ached physically for him. My love burned within me, at times threatening to consume me completely. And though my physical injuries from the termination had healed well, I carried the memory of that day like an open wound. I felt it was visible to everyone I met, marking me out and exposing my secret. The termination was an intense sorrow, woven with shame, which scorched through me day after day. *How can people not see it?* I wondered. Perhaps, I reasoned, they could, and they were shunning me because of it.

You're worthless, I told myself. *First you let the caretaker abuse you, then your grandad, and you accepted pennies in return. Then you let Fred West abuse you. And now you've lost your own child. You're no good, Kathleen Ryan. No good at all.*

As my original due date for giving birth drew nearer, I refused to leave my bedroom. One morning, after a sleepless night, I lay in bed feeling utterly hopeless. Sharp reminders of the past cut through my consciousness. Fragments of memories crowded into my mind, each one a jagged shard of glass. Fred's fleshy face took shape in my imagination, and I heard again his rich glottal accent and his inane giggle: *Come on girlie, I'll show you what I've got in my pants.*

No, I pleaded, pressing my face into the pillow. *Go away. Leave me alone.*

I could feel him there, as real as if he were in the bed, pressing himself against me. I saw his crooked teeth and his dark, bottomless eyes. I reeled at the foul stench oozing from his clothes. Stumbling from the bedroom, I went downstairs to the kitchen. Danny was at work and so the house was empty. Flinging open a cupboard, I picked out a jar of painkillers and filled a glass with water. I swallowed the tablets in handfuls, gulping them down, as though death could not come quickly enough. After the last tablet was gone, I rinsed my glass under the tap, dried it and put it back in the cupboard. Even now, with the end of my life approaching, I felt compelled to leave the kitchen clean and tidy. I allowed myself a sombre smile. Was this what my life amounted to – a life governed by a toxic cycle of abuse and cleaning? And, in the end, the abuse had triumphed.

I traipsed back to bed, expecting to float away into blissful unconsciousness. Instead, the memories kept on coming, like bullets fired against the lining of my eyes. I felt Fred's arms around me, squeezing my buttocks, lifting me off the floor. I remembered him pressing me into the wall while he groped my breasts. Worst of all, I relived the moment where I had woken and found him in my bed. And all the while his squashed face, menacing and moronic in equal measure, loomed over me, just inches away.

Why? I asked silently. *Why did you choose me? Why did you do it?*

Because you're worthless, girlie, laughed the disembodied head. *But you know that already. Course you do.*

His thick hair fell over his forehead and, as he laughed, he opened his mouth wide, the smell of his breath hitting the back of my throat. A relentless tide of memories washed over me, as Fred's peculiar smell hung in the air around my bed. Once again, I was plunged headlong back to Cromwell Street, reliving each horrible, invasive attack. This was 3-D horror, vivid and sharp. In my drugged-up haze, I suddenly had a moment of absolute clarity, and I felt, beyond question, that this man was evil. Fred laughed louder and louder, his spittle wet on my face, and it became a sort of tinny, buzzing sound. The noise was unbearable. I wanted to clap my hands over my ears but somehow my arms were pinned to my sides, exactly as if he had me in his grip, as he had so many times before. Would I ever be free of him? Even as I was dying, he was taking centre stage, playing to the audience, like the clown he so expertly pretended to be. Then over the buzzing noise, I heard footsteps in the distance, big and heavy as though they belonged to a giant. And, behind Fred's large head, I saw my brother standing in the doorway.

'Kathleen!' he yelled. 'Kathleen! What's the matter? Why are you screaming?'

I wasn't even aware I had been screaming, but I couldn't reply. The buzzing was too intense. I felt Danny shaking me, trying to sit me up in bed. But all the time, Fred's face hung like a decapitated ghost between us.

'Please, Kathy,' Danny said. 'Please talk to me.'

And deep within me, the small kernel of hope that had carried me through the worst of my life suddenly stirred and glimmered. I remembered kind Diane, and her fairy-tale wedding. I thought of friendly Sally and her perfect dolls. There was warmth in my heart. And I knew I did not want to die.

'I took an overdose,' I mumbled, unsure if he would hear me above Fred's hideous laughter and the interminable buzzing. 'I need to go to hospital, Danny. Please.'

Danny ran to call an ambulance and came back to the bedroom.

'Help is on the way,' he said. 'Just hold on. What have you taken? Why did you do it? Tell me, Kathy.'

His voice was a distant rope, lassoing me to safety. But the buzzing was louder than ever and now Fred was gripping my arms and lifting me into the air. I was speechless with terror as he flung me back down onto the bed and loosened the belt on his trousers.

Oh, girlie, he sneered. *You will love this. You know you will.*

*

The next time I awoke, I was in a hospital room with a crippling headache and a throat so sore I could barely swallow.

'You've had your stomach pumped, my love,' said a nurse as she straightened my blanket. 'You're safe now. But don't you go doing anything silly again.'

In between running to the toilet to vomit, I lay motionless in bed with a pressure like a metal bar crushing my chest. I was winded by the weight of the shame. I did not want to die. But, I realised, I did not want to live, either. I just wanted all my memories to go away. I needed a clean slate, a magic pill to wipe away the first nineteen years of my life. For none of it, I felt, had been worth keeping and remembering. Not a single moment. Memories flickered like magic candles, relighting each time I thought I had extinguished them: shivering on my way to school in my damp and smelly uniform; rooting in the bins for food; scraping chewing gum from the pavement. Giving my hand to the caretaker, accepting the penny, choosing the chocolate maca-roon. Visiting my grandad, accepting the abuse without question, feeling grateful – and here I choked – *grateful* for a single boiled potato. Fred West, grabbing, groping, squeezing me. His hateful breath. His gormless smile. Fred and Rose, pulling me off the street, dragging me down the stairs, pinning me on the sofa. *It's only a game . . . Oh, girlie, this is what you deserve.*

All day and all night I vomited. As I hung my head over the toilet, I wished I could flush out the bad memories along with the contents of my stomach. The following day, I was weary from despair and lack of sleep. Mid-morning, a psychiatrist came to speak with me.

'Why did you do it?' he asked, peering over his spectacles, a clipboard in his hands.

I didn't know how to even start to answer that, and I just shrugged.

'Will you do it again?' he asked.

I shrugged for a second time and, with a sigh, he walked out of the room. But the next day, he was back.

'Why did you do it?' he asked again, squinting over the same spectacles and carrying the same clipboard.

I stared back, my mouth dry, my tongue so swollen I felt I could not formulate any reply. As I shrugged my shoulders, he turned and left.

By his third visit, I realised he wasn't going to give up until I cooperated. In a few clipped sentences, with my head down, I told him a little about the caretaker and my grandad and my landlord.

'I let it happen,' I mumbled, through parched lips. 'It was my fault. And then I had a termination. My baby was the only good thing ever to happen to me and I let him down. I can never forgive myself.'

The psychiatrist smiled briskly. 'It's best to move on from all of that,' he said, ticking a few boxes on his clipboard. 'Forget about it now and leave it in the past.'

Bewildered, I said nothing. But simmering under the surface, I felt so angry with myself for opening up to a doctor who clearly had no idea how I felt and no real interest in my recovery. Once again, I had let myself down. I had made another bad decision. What was wrong with me?

The psychiatrist cleared his throat and asked, 'And are you going to do it again, Kathleen?'

'No,' I replied wearily.

He ticked a final box on his clipboard and then told me I could go home later that day. I had no bag to pack, no fresh clothes to change into, no get-well cards or flowers to wrap. I called Danny from the ward payphone and he offered to meet me after work. While I waited, a cleaner, around the same age as my mother, came bustling into the room. She had such a jolly manner that she seemed to glow. Yet it failed to cheer me up at all.

'Listen, pet,' she said kindly, as she swept under the bed. 'I know it's none of my business, but you're young and beautiful and you have your whole life ahead of you. If this is over a young man, and it usually is, you need to forget him. He's not worth it and there are plenty more fish in the sea. Things will get better, pet. I promise you that.'

She obviously knew why I was in hospital and though she had no idea of the demons that stalked my mind, I understood she was only trying to help. It meant so much me, that small kindness. She could not have known how I would cling to those words and repeat them over and over. In the months to come, I carried her compassion, like a tiny jewel, in my pocket. Every now and again, I got it out for a polish and watched it shine.

Things will get better, pet. I promise you that.

Late that afternoon, Danny arrived to collect me and suggested we go to the cafe in Woolworths for a cup of tea and a snack.

'My treat,' he said.

Normally, I'd have been thrilled with the idea of eating out, but I could not face the thought of food. The inside of my stomach felt like it had been rubbed raw with sandpaper. Instead, I sipped my tea and watched Danny eat his sandwich.

'Look, you can't try that again,' he said. 'You can't carry on like this.'

159

I nodded miserably. 'I know.'

'Why did you do it?' he asked. 'What's wrong?'

I remembered, as a small child, telling my mother about my grandad's abuse, and in my mind's eye I could still see the soap suds flying as she accused me of telling lies. I also thought of the effort it had been to confide in the psychiatrist and how useless and trite his advice had been. I had learned my lesson. I would not make the mistake of telling anyone else ever again.

'I don't know,' I sighed. 'It was just a silly mistake. I'm sorry. It won't happen again.'

21

Back at home, I found a new job and forced myself into some sort of normality. I suffered with horrendous headaches, which seemed a perverse consequence of taking too many painkillers. But I saw the migraines as my punishment – my reminder, if any were needed, that my behaviour was unforgivable. Mired in despair, I trudged through each day. I hoped a new environment might help my depression, and as soon as I had enough money for the ferry, I booked a crossing to Dublin. Aunty Frances found me a rented room just around the corner from her and I applied for a job in the canteen of a nearby hospital. My grandad had worked in the kitchen of the same hospital for all of his adult life. When I arrived for interview, and the supervisor realised who I was, he waved away the formalities.

'Your grandfather was a great fella,' he said, shaking my hand. 'He worked hard every day of his life, God rest his soul. The job's yours if you want it, Kathleen.'

Though I was pleased to get the job, I'd rather have done so on my own merit and not on the reputation of my abusive grandad. The dissonance between my grandad's public and private behaviour was bewildering. Again, as with Fred West, everyone had seemed to love him. He'd been liked and respected and was much missed by the hospital staff. I was the only person, it seemed, who had an issue with him. And it cemented my belief that I was the one at fault and, moreover, that it was pointless for me ever to speak out about the abuse.

You're worthless, Kathleen. Of course it's your fault.

Pushing my well-worn anxieties aside, I settled in well at work and in my bedsit. My room had a coal fire and, every day, Frances let herself into the flat, raked out the fireplace and laid a new fire, ready for me to come home to in the evening. It was the perfect metaphor for the infusion of warmth she brought into my life. Frances was kindness itself, the closest I would ever come to enjoying a maternal bond. I was too ashamed to confide in her, or in anyone, about the termination. I feared they would view me as harshly as I viewed myself. Yet I think Frances sensed a fragility in me, a deep-seated sadness, which I could not shift or hide. For she took me under her wing, building me that daily fire and inviting me for Sunday lunch every week. I remembered how I used to brush her hair when I was small. Even now, without that physical contact, there was still so much affection between us. On my twenty-first birthday, in January 1981, she took me out shopping for the day and treated me to new underwear.

'You're a beautiful girl, Kathy,' she smiled. 'You deserve the best.'

By the end of that year, I had a new job in a coat factory, different from the one I'd worked in previously. All around me was chaos and chatter and clanking machinery, and I tried to lose myself in it. Each time my thoughts ran down the tracks of my past, I shoved them off course, like a derailed train. *Don't think about it, Kathy*, I told myself sternly. But, oh, if only it were that simple. The abuse weighed me down, and I felt I was carrying ghosts on my back. My memories hung around me like dust particles and, no matter how I cleaned and how I scrubbed my little bedsit, I could not get rid of them. Each time I felt I was moving forward, my past would creep up behind me, catch me in a net and drag me back. And the pair of arms that pulled me back belonged, every time, to Fred West.

In the factory, each day, I'd hear one voice above all the others, singing along to the radio, telling stories or jokes. Like me, Callum worked on the factory floor. He was four years older than me, very thin, with blonde hair and green eyes. From the first time I heard him sing, I fancied him. Yet we were complete opposites – he was outgoing, confident and happy-go-lucky. Perhaps that was why I fell for him, drawn like a moth to a bright light. I was too shy, though, to tell him how I felt, and I didn't for a moment think he would notice me. As my twenty-second birthday approached in January 1982, the other girls at the factory began badgering me to share my plans.

'Are we going out? Drinks, pub crawl, clubbing?' they asked.

I shook my head. 'Oh no, nothing like that,' I said bashfully. 'I don't really celebrate birthdays. I've never had a birthday party in my life.'

'In that case,' they decided, 'you're having one this year.'

Bemused and grateful, I was sidelined as they threw themselves into the organisation. Before I knew it, they'd booked a city centre pub in Dublin and invited most of the factory along.

One of my pals winked. 'Don't worry,' she said. 'Callum's coming.'

I blushed and giggled. Sure enough, he arrived, ready to commandeer the Karaoke. He had a great voice and I swooned as he belted out hit after hit. At the end of the night, he wrote his number on an empty cigarette packet and smiled.

'Call me.'

But though my heart flipped, I had no intention of phoning him, or anyone else. For why would someone like him be interested in someone like me? And by the time I arrived home that night, as was my way, I had completely dismantled the incident and rebuilt it into something different.

'He probably felt he had to give me his number because it was my birthday,' I told myself. 'He was just being polite, as a way of thanking me for the invite.'

A few days later, I was on my way into the factory when I spotted Callum at the gates, stamping his boots against the cold.

'Why didn't you call me?' he asked, blowing on his fingers.

'Dunno,' I replied sheepishly. 'It's freezing, though, isn't it?'

I carried on walking, but he hurried after me and asked for my number. I gave it to him immediately and was glad my cheeks were flushed with cold to hide my blushes. And that same evening, Callum called to arrange our first date for that weekend. My stomach turned somersaults of excitement when I saw him standing outside the door of my bedsit. From that first night, we were rarely apart and, six months on, I fell pregnant. When the test was positive, I felt a rush of conflicting emotions. I was over the moon. And yet, I could not help thinking of the baby I had terminated. I did not deserve a second chance. I did not deserve a baby. The abortion was like a bleeding, weeping lesion inside my heart and I was sure it would prevent me from having a healthy baby. Despite all my fears, the pregnancy went well and Callum and I travelled to Gloucester to get married at the register office, surrounded by our family and friends.

Late in 1983, I went into labour. There were complications with the birth, and I bled heavily, slipping away, but vaguely aware of a panic around me.

When I finally came round, woozy and confused, a doctor said, 'Well, you really went through the mill there. We thought we might lose you.'

Again, I was catapulted back to the termination. This was my punishment, I was sure of it. The only way I could pay for what I had done was with my own life. For days I drifted in and out of consciousness, barely aware that our beautiful baby son, John, lay in a cot beside me. When, one day, I saw his big, wise eyes staring back at me and felt the comforting warmth of him on my chest, I was overcome with a tidal wave of love. I knew then I had to try to put the tragedy of the termination behind me and focus on my little family. Callum and I rented a flat on the outskirts of Dublin, and I was so happy and proud, taking my little boy home from hospital.

'You've made your mammy the happiest girl in the world,' I told him with a smile.

Soon after the birth, I saw a dentist for the very first time in my life. I explained I'd never even owned a toothbrush until I was around eighteen.

'Well, your teeth are looking remarkably good,' he said. 'You must have had a healthy diet as a child.'

I nodded distractedly but, in that moment, I was back in Sadie's sweetshop, a penny in my warm hand as I agonised between chocolate drops and chews. What lengths I had gone to, what suffering I had endured, for a single sweet.

'Yes,' I replied quietly. 'I suppose I did.'

With my own child to love now, I wanted to look only forward. I tried to clear my mind of the past, in the same way I might clear a room of clutter. But my brain was jammed with unwelcome memories and reminders. Watching my son grow was a blessing but it also laid bare the failings of my own childhood. My own parents had had challenges of their own and I did not blame them. Nevertheless, I was determined not to repeat their mistakes. And with the spectre of the abuse hovering over me like one of my father's smoke rings, I became fiercely protective and vigilant. I never let my little boy out of my sight. I didn't like leaving him with babysitters, or even relatives, because of course one of my abusers had come from inside my family circle.

'I'd rather just look after John myself,' I told Callum.

But though motherhood was filled with the biggest worries, it was also the biggest blessing, and I was keen to have another baby as soon as I could.

But it was seven years before our daughter, Jess, was born. She was beautiful – more than perfect in every way.

'Hello darling,' I murmured, holding her cheek to mine.

But later, as I changed her in the hospital, I noticed a speck of blood in her nappy. Instantly, I froze. This was payback time, I told myself. I had terminated one child. So now I must lose one. This was to be the retribution. My mind raced away with itself, looping round and back again, with unthinkable possibilities.

'Please, no,' I pleaded silently. 'Punish me, don't punish my baby girl.'

I was so frightened, I didn't dare even mention the blood to a doctor. It was only when Frances visited that afternoon, and asked me what was wrong, that I broke down in tears.

'Oh, Kathy, it's nothing to worry about,' she said. 'I've seen this before.'

She bustled off to find a paediatrician and, after a full examination, Jess was declared completely healthy. I wept tears of gratitude for the gift of my precious girl, feeling, once again, I had somehow escaped disaster. Right from the start, Jess's personality shone through. She was a jolly, smiley baby, full of energy and curiosity, and she had bags of the confidence I so thoroughly lacked. I was overjoyed that my children were being raised with a spirit and self-assurance I had only ever dreamed of.

22

When Jess was three years old, Callum and I split. We had been too young when we first got together, and we were wildly different. In truth, I found physical intimacy difficult and stressful. In bed, I was bombarded by images of the caretaker's rubbery Thing, of Fred West's doughy face, of the cold penny in my warm hand. For me, sex was about control, pain and shame. I could not shake that, could not leave that curse behind, no matter how I tried. And so, with Jess in her buggy and John clutching my hand, I boarded the ferry from Dun Laoghaire to Holyhead. Gloucester held many bad memories for me, but my closest friends and family were there. Mam allowed us to stay with her for two weeks, as she was living back in Gloucester after yet another move. Then, with the help of my best pal, Jane, I found a cheap rented house with two bedrooms. She and I had met a couple of years earlier when she married my cousin and we had been firm friends ever since. Jane rallied round our circle of friends and they sent odd pieces of equipment and furniture.

Someone sent a pair of dining chairs, another sent a drying rack, a neighbour gifted me a single mattress. The rest I cobbled together from charity shops. I relied on my social security money at first and then quickly found work as a cleaner. While John was at school, I worked hard, taking Jess along with me to the offices where I cleaned. I preferred to keep her close to me at all times; I knew only too well that predators were everywhere, and wickedness skulked in the most unexpected places.

Once, while still a toddler, Jess developed a stubborn rash that refused to clear up. I had, since childhood, been afflicted with the belief that educated people were better than I was, and I was particularly hesitant about speaking with doctors, teachers or police officers. Yet knowing Jess needed medical attention, I took her along for a doctor's appointment. I was already tongue-tied and nervous but when I saw the GP was male, my anxiety skyrocketed.

Reminders of the caretaker and my grandad flashed into my mind as the doctor said, 'Can you undress her please so I can look at the rash?'

I felt so uncomfortable, but I could not possibly explain to him why. It was difficult enough for me simply to describe the rash. Somehow, I mumbled my way through the consultation and, a few minutes later, walking out of the surgery with a prescription, I felt no sense of achievement, simply a prevailing sense of shame. I was not good enough to talk to these people. Time and time again, I avoided seeing the doctor or chatting with the children's teachers because I felt it was not my place.

These misgivings were only small blots on what was otherwise such a happy time, raising a young family. I spoiled the children, working overtime so that John could have a karate uniform and

Jess could have a sparkly leotard and dance shoes. My cupboards were bursting with goodies and my home was sparklingly clean and always warm. Birthdays and Christmas were huge events with cakes, presents and parties. If ever I had a dilemma regarding my children, I would ask myself what my own parents would have done in the same situation – and then resolutely do the opposite. Despite my troubled upbringing, I had a measure of sympathy for my parents, especially my mother. They had been raised in a different era and without the necessary skills or finances to be the parents they might have liked to be. Yet I knew that cycle had to be broken, and it started with me. I was overjoyed to be a mother, I appreciated the responsibility and I understood I had to show my children a different way. If I could have wrapped the moon and presented it to them, I would have gladly done so.

Early one evening in February 1994, I was busy chopping onions for a chicken curry and singing along to the radio. We had only been in our new place for a few months but we were really starting to settle in. John loved school and Jess had a place at nursery, and I could work longer hours. It had been a huge wrench to leave Jess in the care of strangers, but she loved it there. Little by little, our house was becoming a home, and a happy one, too.

The music on the radio stopped and the hourly news came on. The first item was about a search for human remains at a house in Gloucester. I felt the usual fleeting pang of sympathy for the victim before reaching into the fridge for the garlic.

The newsreader continued, 'Police have confirmed that Frederick West, aged fifty-two, and his forty-year-old wife Rosemary, of 25 Cromwell Street, have been arrested on suspicion of multiple murders.'

'What?' I gasped, as the garlic fell from my hands to the floor. 'What did you say?'

I half expected the man on the radio to reply and reassure me it was all a big misunderstanding.

'What?' I stammered again.

In a daze I ran through to the living room, flinging cushions onto the floor and upending the coffee table as I looked for the TV remote control. The floor seemed to tilt beneath me. My foundations were crumbling and falling away and the world was collapsing around me. My heart thudded as I flicked through the channels and, suddenly, there it was: 25 Cromwell Street staring back at me, at once familiar and yet absurdly foreign. In a flash, I was blasted back into my teenage years, standing on the side path, lifting the pram out through the front door. It was a scene of ordinary and safe domesticity. And yet now, as a white police tent and cordon fluttered in the wind, the place looked hostile and sinister. *The house of horror.* With shaking hands, I dialled Deirdre's number. She answered immediately, and before I could speak, she whispered: 'I know.'

We stayed on the line in complete silence, except for the sound of us both weeping softly. There was so much for us to say that, conversely, we said nothing at all. The call seemed to last for ever until eventually I heard Jess wake from her nap upstairs and call for me.

'I'll have to go,' I mumbled.

Numb with shock, I ended the call and continued making the curry. But my mind was a whirl of emotion. As the months had gone on, at Cromwell Street, I had disliked Fred and Rose West more and more. At times I had been wary, frightened even. But at no point had I feared for my life. It had never once occurred to me that Fred could be a killer. I remembered his gormless grin, his fake limp, his silly giggle. Was there really a cold-blooded serial killer behind that clown mask? No matter how many news reports I heard, no matter how often it was repeated that evening on every TV channel, on every radio station, I just could not believe it. Though I had nothing to back up my theory, Fred seemed the very opposite of what I imagined a killer to be. But while I had never suspected Rose of murder, or anything close to it, I had to admit something about her had unsettled me. There was a darkness and a strangeness about her. And I was now beginning to understand that her soul was rotten and fetid to the core.

Murder? I asked myself, over and over. *Murder?*

I didn't sleep at all that night. Snippets of memory, one pushing past the next, jostled for position in my mind. Fred pressing me against the wall. Fred climbing into my bed. Fred offering free rent in return for sexual favours. In context, these incidents were now terrifying. But what scared me more was reliving the moment he and Rose had taken my arms and tried to drag me back into the house. At the time, I'd been scared that Fred might sexually assault me. But, looking back through the prism of their arrests, that incident was revealed for what it was – an attempted kidnap. Was that the point at which they had tried to snare me? And what about the time, I shuddered, when they had dragged me downstairs into their living room, Fred shoving his crotch into my face and Rose stroking my hair? My heart raced as I remembered my lucky escape when the doorbell rang. My skin prickled with the realisation that I had come close, so close, to becoming another victim. Yet overriding all thoughts, all flashbacks, was Shirley. Poor Shirley. I had never truly believed she was in Germany. Now, I had to face the possibility that she had been savagely murdered.

'Please, no,' I whispered, as the tears streamed down my cheeks. 'Not Shirley.'

I didn't have to wait long to find out. The story was covered voraciously in every newspaper and on every TV and radio channel. And a few days later, as I was ironing school uniforms, a newsflash confirmed that the dismembered body of eighteen-year-old Shirley Robinson had been found buried in the back garden of Cromwell Street. The sharp tang of bile hit my throat as it constricted with a rush of vomit. I dashed to the toilet with my head thumping and a blinding white light flashing behind my eyes. Slumping onto the bathroom tiles, I waited for my seizure to pass, each tremor rolling through me like a silent scream. This was worse than I could ever have imagined. Not only had he murdered Shirley, but he had buried her right there, in the back garden, and in pieces, under our bedroom window. She'd been afforded little respect or dignity in life, and none at all in death. There was no mention on the news of Shirley being heavily pregnant, but I feared her baby had died with her. As I came around from the seizure, I pictured the lonely bag of baby clothes, still waiting in the bedroom for all I knew, and a strangled sob escaped my throat. How could anyone do this to another human being? I had a nauseating recollection of Fred digging in the garden and banging in the cellar. *Always busy with a DIY project. Always helping out.*

'Maybe he's digging a swimming pool,' we had laughed.

I cringed at our naivety, clapping my hands over my face to block my vision. For while we had stood at the window and wondered where Shirley had gone, Fred was openly digging her grave below us, waving and chuckling as though he hadn't a care in the world. On those warm summer nights, when we had flung open our window for fresh air, he was burying her corpse just a few feet away. The place was not a garden; it was a graveyard. I had no idea how or why Shirley had died. But it beggared belief that he would murder not only her, but his own unborn child as well. Alongside the barbarity, I was staggered by Fred's audacity and his tangled tales of deception. He had told such convincing stories of Shirley vanishing without trace, of her 'moving on'. I remembered his little shrug and his smile, as though it was just one of those things. Then came the story about her having gone to Germany. All the while, she was just feet away, dead in the cold, hard earth. Aside from the obvious wickedness, I would never have credited Fred with such guile. I was astonished. I called Deirdre and again, we sat in silence, listening to each other's breathing. The horrors we shared were too awful to say out loud. But it was a small comfort to know that she was there.

The police searches continued, each day bringing with it fresh anguish. More dismembered bodies were found. More broken bones. More broken hearts. At televised press conferences, officers explained they were working painstakingly to piece the body parts together. It was like a sadistic jigsaw. I thought of Fred hammering and sawing for hours on end and everything fell sickeningly into place. He was not a DIY fan. He was a butcher. A butcher of people.

I read that the police inquiry had started, not in relation to Shirley, but to investigate the disappearance of Heather West, Fred and Rosemary's eldest daughter. When police started digging in the garden of 25 Cromwell Street, they had found

Heather's remains first. I remembered the girl who had come out of the living room when Fred was squeezing me in the hallway.

Meet your new friend, Kathy!

I saw her face on the evening news, and I was struck by the strong likeness to her father, the dark hair and heavy eyebrows, and I felt sure it was the same child.

'You poor girl,' I whispered.

There were no words for how she had suffered. Shirley's remains were found after Heather's, with reports claiming a single femur had been found initially. The thought of Shirley's delicate frame, and her neat pregnancy bump, hacked into pieces, was horrific. I did not, could not, allow myself to think of what had happened to her baby. Next, police found remains of a girl later identified as Alison Chambers, a lodger who had arrived at Cromwell Street just a few weeks before we left. I didn't remember her, but the parallels screamed back at me. I was, I conceded, so very nearly their next prey.

'Oh, Kathy, it could have been you,' said Deirdre, echoing my fears the next time we spoke. 'I keep thinking of the way he used to grab you. He was grooming you. You could have been the next one if you hadn't left when you did. You had such a lucky escape.'

But I didn't feel at all lucky. I felt guilty. Why had I survived when all those girls had not? Why Shirley – and why not me? The shame was like a funeral drum, beating relentlessly against the insides of my skull.

It should have been you, it should have been you, it should have been you.

Perhaps I had been next on the list, as Deirdre suggested, and I had been spared only because we had fled the house that morning. Maybe I had been spared purely due to logistics. But then I thought of how our mother had called round to Cromwell Street, most weeks, on her way to the shops. She had only ever tapped at the front door and stayed for a few moments. I don't think she ever even stepped inside the house. But her presence was, perhaps, enough to put Fred off. My mother's visits were a clear warning that, should Deirdre or I disappear, someone would notice. My mother was not involved in our lives to the point where I could confide in her that I was being abused or attacked. And maybe Fred realised that, too; he sensed I was fair game, but only up to a point. He could see that in me, as surely as if I wore a placard around my neck, I am sure of it. I was scared, vulnerable and damaged and he recognised those signs only too well, as this was his particular area of twisted expertise. But my mother would certainly notice if I vanished. Shirley had nobody. Many of those poor girls had nobody. I had somebody. And, to this day, I believe that saved me. There have been many problems between my mother and me over the years. I have always longed for a closer bond. I have always yearned for what we have never had. But I am eternally grateful for her spot-check visits at Cromwell Street. I owe her my life.

23

Meanwhile, with daily reports of yet more searches and more bones, the size of the investigation grew and grew. Police announced they were working with other forces throughout the UK and also with police officers in Holland, Germany and Switzerland in an effort to identify possible victims. There were reports that the remains of a poor girl named Lynda Gough had been found in the Cromwell Street garden. Then came news that Fred West had confessed to more murders. I was dumbfounded. How had this happened? How had he gone undetected, unchallenged, for so long? I included myself in this criticism. I should have known; I should have sensed it somehow. I should have done something. I had lived, side by side, with Britain's worst serial killers, and I hadn't suspected a thing. Like an invisible cloak, weighted with lead, I carried the blame for this, just as I did for the abuse in my childhood and for the termination of my baby.

Despite the chaos in my head, I did my best to continue as

though nothing was wrong. Nobody except my pal Jane knew I'd been a lodger at Cromwell Street, and I was anxious it should stay that way. I tried to avoid the gossip and the news reports as much as I could. But it was impossible – the story was constantly on the telly, the radio and across every newsstand. The details seemed to permeate the air around me as though carried on the wind. Cromwell Street, and my time there, felt like a sinister intruder, casting a dark shadow at my door. My mother had moved back to Derby again and she called me, her voice trembling with shock as she discussed the arrests.

'They seemed like such nice, normal people,' she gasped. 'I can't believe my own daughters were living with serial killers.'

Throughout March the press reported that the remains of four more young women, all former lodgers, had been found at the address. Therese Siegenthaler had been discovered hidden in concrete in a false fireplace in the cellar. Shirley Hubbard was found under the cellar floor. Juanita Mott had been found under a staircase in the cellar and Lucy Partington had been found in the cellar. Each announcement left me reeling; numb and stupefied. We had lived in that house, we had eaten, slept, laughed and cried. We had made cheese on toast, we had handwashed our clothes, we had pushed pebbles into the peepholes. For over a year, we had called it home. Yet we were surrounded by dead bodies, under the floors, behind the staircases and outside our window. We had lived in a real-life horror film, with the enemies right in our midst. And it still wasn't over. A few days later, another body, belonging to a young woman called Carol Ann Cooper, was found in the cellar. Catherine West, Fred West's first wife, was found buried in a field. All of the victims were young and female and either lodgers at Cromwell Street or family members of Fred West.

There were more lurid headlines when Fred appeared at Gloucester Magistrates' Court on eight separate charges of murder and was remanded in custody to Gloucester Prison. And still it went on, like the longest nightmare. At the end of March, digging began at a second address, a house on Midland Road in Gloucester, where Fred and Rose had once lived. The following month, inquests into the deaths of the women were opened and adjourned. Late in April, I was shattered to read that Rose West had been charged with the murders of Lynda Gough, Carol Ann Cooper, Lucy Partington and Therese Siegenthaler. In the back of my mind, I suppose I had somehow shifted the responsibility for the murders onto Fred. It was true, I had sensed venom in Rose. But I could not believe that a woman, herself a mother, could be capable of such raw violence and bloodshed. The shocks continued, each a thunderclap. I felt as though every time I came up for air, my head was thrust back underwater with yet another revelation. I was drowning in the sheer shock of it all.

In May 1994, Rose West was charged with the murders of Shirley Hubbard, Juanita Mott and Shirley Robinson. Later that month, the remains of Charmaine West, Fred's daughter from a previous relationship, were found under the kitchen window at the address on Midland Road. She had been, poignantly, just eight years old. Sadness washed through me when I saw her grainy photo on the news, her innocent little face peering back at me. Again, I asked myself how this had happened. I felt I was losing faith in all of humanity. Still the death toll rose, each a punch to the gut, as excavations and digging continued. In June, the remains of Ann McFall were found in Fingerpost Field, Herefordshire. Like Shirley, she was eighteen years old and eight months pregnant with Fred's child when she died.

The scandal of the Cromwell Street murders travelled right around the world and ghoulish tragedy hunters travelled for hundreds of miles to visit the scene. It became a sort of tourist shrine, and I loathed it. It seemed so disrespectful to Shirley and to all the other young victims. After all they had suffered, surely they deserved privacy and respect in death. For some reason, I kept on thinking of the bag of baby clothes that Deirdre had collected for Shirley. All those months, we had saved the bag, hoping that she might come back with her new baby. The tragic irony was that she had been there all the time. She and her baby were outside our window and the poor little mite would never need those clothes. Irrationally, I wanted to bury one of the little outfits with them, when they were finally and formally laid to rest. Just a small scrap of humanity, a reminder that someone cared, in the midst of unspeakable pain. The disparity was agonising – the innocence of the tiny blue baby jackets, the milky scent of a newborn baby, set against the evil of the murders. I hated the attitudes in the press and in some of the public, treating Shirley as if she was no longer a person, a teenager, a mother to be. Someone with a shy smile and a love of red ice lollies. She had become simply a victim, dehumanised by her own death and more so by the manner of it. My focus on the baby clothes was, I suppose, a pitiful attempt to make her real again. To make her matter.

Locally, too, the murders were all anyone talked about. They were the sole topic of conversation in the supermarket, at the school gates and at work. Still I gave no hint that I had been a lodger at Cromwell Street and listened to the exclamations in silence, desperate to correct the wild gossip, but keen to stay out of the whole mess.

'I heard there was a head and shoulders in the bath,' someone announced in the post office queue. 'No body. Just head and shoulders.'

And in the shop one day, a man made a crass joke about Fred West's favourite lager being Tennent's.

'Tennent's, tenants!' he grinned. 'He loves to get the Tennent's in. Don't you get it?'

With a frozen face, I glared at him. I could not smile but neither could I tell anyone what I knew. For me, there was no lighter aspect to this and there never would be. Others, I'd heard, had given the police names of young women who had lodged at Cromwell Street and subsequently vanished. The sheer numbers of missing people were mind blowing and, again, I felt my belief in humanity draining away. What kind of world did we live in?

It was widely thought that the police were overwhelmed by the size and status of the investigation, and they did not have limitless funds available to search for a rapidly growing list of missing people. Reports in the press said Gloucester police had applied to the Home Office for £651,000 of assistance, but their request was later refused.

'I knew a young girl who lived at Cromwell Street, and she hasn't been seen since,' one of my neighbours told me one morning. 'I just always thought she'd moved away. But that place was like a Bermuda Triangle for troubled young women. They went in, they never came out. She could be under the patio for all I know.'

I made a sympathetic sound and hurried into my house. I felt like a fraud, pretending I'd never lived there. Yet I couldn't have coped with all the attention. I couldn't even make sense of what had happened myself, let alone allow other people to pick over it in public. I worried too that people would blame me, as I blamed myself. What if they held me responsible because I had survived, and the others had not? What right did I have to be alive? And what if – even worse – they blamed me for not telling the police about Fred West? A voice in my head, cold with judgement, reminded me that if I had reported the sexual assaults, he might have been sent to prison. And Shirley might have been saved. I was dragged down by the weight of this responsibility, bent double with shame and regret. Could I, should I, have stopped him? I did not see myself as a victim, with my own trauma and my own fears. I only saw my faults. And the root of it all lay in that moment when, aged eight, I had accepted a sweet from a caretaker who sexually abused me. I had blamed myself that day and I had not stopped since. I took responsibility for the Wests' abhorrent behaviour just as I did for everything else.

It should have been you. It should have been you. It should have been you.

The stories continued, a drip-feed of horror, and though they made me physically ill, I was gripped by each revelation. And while I was desperate to distance myself, I knew I was right at the centre of it. I deserved blame and judgement. Irrationally, I held myself responsible for everything, every revelation, every new detail. And as the accusations flew around my head, I sank lower and lower. I was so thankful for my two children, their bright light pulling me through those dark troughs and giving me a reason to smile.

24

My usual routine after the school and nursery run was to nip back home for a cup of tea before work. I might even run the hoover around the hallway and rinse the breakfast dishes before I left to start my cleaning shift. But one summer morning, without consciously making the decision, I found myself standing at the end of Cromwell Street. Though the excavations had finished, there was a police car parked outside, with a single officer guarding the side path to the front door. The house itself was cordoned off, and I stood well back, blending in with the early-morning rush hour. My skin crawled with revulsion as I slowly lifted my head to look at the house.

The windows, blank and dark, were like hollowed-out eyes. The curly white sign on the house, '25 Cromwell Street', had been removed. It seemed a mockery now, a sick joke. The whole building heaved with the secrets of the dead. Was it ready to spew out more, or clasp them closer inside the walls? I could not tell. But I fancied I could see Shirley leaning on the fence, with her red ice lolly and her neat little bump under her old-fashioned floral dress. In my mind's eye I saw Fred, too, whistling and giggling as he carried his DIY tools – his murder tools – down to the cellar. And there was Rose, reclining on her chair, with her haughty glare and her nasty temper. It had seemed to me that everything was exposed when she wore her see-through negligee to lure me into her living room. Little did I know how many more horrible secrets there were, snapping like alligators and lurking beneath the cheap nylon. But even now, under the glare of the media spotlight, the place looked so ordinary, so benign. Moving in here that November day, I'd felt safe; reassured and cheered by the family unit – Mum, Dad and a gaggle of kids. The names, the abbreviations, Fred and Rose, had sounded friendly and approachable. I had been so convincingly sucked in. Yet I was not the only one. They had got away with murder, year after year after year. Maybe, if I had stayed, they'd have got away with mine too.

Despite the early-morning sunshine, I was beginning to shiver as I stood motionless on the pavement. And on the breeze, I caught a sudden whiff of a stomach-turning stench, that horribly familiar smell that had seemed to seep from Fred's pores. I'd likened it, sometimes, to the rotting flesh of dead animals. Now with sickening clarity I knew it was dead humans. He was drenched in the dried blood and bone marrow of his victims. With a gasp, I turned and hurried away. Perhaps I had hoped for some sort of closure or peace in returning to Cromwell Street, but I found none. I trudged home, feeling heavier than ever.

In October 1994, and again in November, Fred and Rose West appeared before Gloucester Magistrates' Court. Remanded into custody each time, they were instructed to appear again for committal proceedings in February 1995. There was a feeding frenzy from the world outside, an insatiable appetite for any crumbs of information, any detail, no matter how small. The demand scared me and only drove my secrets deeper still. A voice in my head reminded me that I was at the heart of this, and I had a story to share. I was agonisingly aware of the inverse correlation of burying my own trauma further as the Wests' secrets were being uncovered. And if I could have spoken out, I would have. But I might as well have had a zip across my mouth. I felt winded with shock. It was a tragedy of massive proportions, and I was consumed by a miasma of revulsion, self-reproach, anger and sadness. Even at night, I could not escape. I had vivid nightmares where Shirley screamed my name from the back garden. I tried to run from the bedroom to help her but, when I opened the door, Fred was there, laughing, with a knife in his hands and blood dripping from his crooked teeth. He had transmogrified into a smiling devil dog. It even looked as though his hands were covered by dark fur. Terrified, I slammed the door shut and hid myself away in the bedroom, under the scratchy green blanket. I did not go to help Shirley and, eventually, her screams died away. When I woke, the guilt was so intense that I was pinned to my bed. Paralysed by shame.

The children and I enjoyed a quiet Christmas that year, and I spoiled them, perhaps even a little more than usual, with piles of treats and gifts. The Cromwell Street murders continued to pollute my thoughts, but they were also a lesson in the fragility of life. I vowed to enjoy each precious moment with my children, protecting them from the worry and the sadness in the world for as long as I could. After Christmas, Deirdre came to visit for the day with her family, but we didn't say a word about the murders.

But when she left, she took me in her arms, and said: 'You mustn't feel guilty, Kathy. None of this was our fault.'

My children were too young to enjoy New Year's Eve and so we didn't really celebrate, and I enjoyed an early night with a good book and a cup of tea. On the evening of New Year's Day 1995, as I was tidying away festive debris, I switched on the radio.

The newsreader's voice boomed out into my living room: 'Fred West, the "House Of Horrors" builder facing twelve murder charges, has been found dead in his prison cell. Prison staff discovered him hanging from strips of clothing at Winson Green Prison near Birmingham earlier today. Attempts to save him failed and he was declared dead by medical staff at one-thirty p.m. It is believed he committed suicide.'

My immediate feeling was of relief, cleansing my mind, like a salve.

Good, he's gone, I said to myself. *He's gone from the earth.*

It felt like the end of a plague, or the extinction of a killer species. Reflexively, I reached for the phone and dialled Deirdre's number. From the way she whimpered when she answered, I knew she knew too. For a while we sat quietly, our silence loaded with emotion, tremors of shock passing down the line and back again.

'I am so glad he's dead,' I said eventually.

'Yes, but think of all those poor girls who will never get justice,' Deirdre replied angrily. 'Think of their families. He's taken the coward's way out. He's escaped.'

'You're right,' I conceded. 'The families deserve the truth.'

But I was still glad he was dead, and I could not change how I felt. The world was a safer and a better place without him. And, in my troubled dreams, when I felt Fred's hands slithering under my clothes, I opened my mouth wide and yelled: 'You can't hurt me! You're dead now!'

But my protestations did not stop my nightmares, nor did they stop Fred's wandering hands. His eyes held the same sinister menace as before. My dreams of Shirley upset me more than ever: she always needed help – drowning, sinking, injured in a car crash, locked outside without a key. And in those dreams, just as in life, I was unable to save her. I thought of Shirley every day. I spoke to her, too, explaining myself over and over, in a desperate search for an absolution I knew she could not give and I felt I did not deserve.

'I'm sorry, Shirley,' I mumbled. 'I'm sorry. I really am.'

In the weeks afterwards, Fred's suicide note was published in the press and, though every bone in my body screamed out against me reading it, I felt compelled to do so. Perhaps foolishly, I hoped for signs of remorse or regret. His deluded letter was filled with narcissistic rambling and it was further confirmation, if any were needed, that he was a ruthless, heartless monster:

To Rose West, Steve and Mae, Well Rose it's your birthday on 29 November 1994 and you will be 41 and still beautiful and still lovely and I love you. We will always be in love. The most wonderful thing in my life was when I met you. Our love is special to us. So, love, keep your promises to me. You know what they are. Where we are put together for ever and ever is up to you. We loved Heather, both of us. I would love Charmaine to be with Heather and Rena. You will always be

Mrs. West, all over the world. That is important to me and to you. I haven't got you a present, but all I have is my life. I will give it to you, my darling. When you are ready, come to me. I will be waiting for you.

In disgust, I ripped the newspaper into shreds and threw it in the outside dustbin. I couldn't bear to have his poison in my home.

In February, Rose West appeared for committal at Dursley Magistrates' Court. By now she had also been charged with the murder of her young stepdaughter, Charmaine. She was facing ten charges of murder. On the news, I saw images of the prison van being pelted with eggs by furious onlookers.

Oh, that won't bother her, I said to myself. *Not one bit.*

I pictured her sitting in the van, with her hooded eyes and her imperious sideways stare. A few eggs would have no impact on her rotten heart. Remembering the way she had stroked my hair, her lips so close to my cheek, I retched. She could not have been closer to me. And I, in turn, could not have been closer to death.

Cromwell Street felt like a sharp blade, snipping away at the fabric of my family. But I knew I could not let it rip me apart completely. Day to day, my unease had to be packaged up and thrust aside. Like any single mum, I juggled looking after my children, running my home and earning a wage. By now, I had a new job, working in residential homes, mainly caring for the elderly. It was a role I loved, and I soon realised I wanted to make this my career. I did every course, every training day that was offered to me, determined to make something of myself. I even went to college in the evenings. Later I moved onto working with young children with additional needs, both physical and emotional. I gained more qualifications – in health and social care – and I was eventually promoted to team leader. It was a proud day, starting my new job, with a team of workers relying on me for guidance and advice. For a girl with little education and even less self-belief, I had come a long way.

25

Around six weeks after Fred West's suicide, I opened the door to find a police officer outside.

'I understand you were a lodger at 25 Cromwell Street with Frederick and Rosemary West,' he said. 'I'd like to come in and ask you some questions.'

Shocked and flustered, I could only blush crimson and stare at him, as though I was a child caught out for telling a fib. My mind raced, wondering how on earth he'd tracked me down, especially after all this time. Possibly, I was on the electoral roll for those fourteen months at Cromwell Street. Or maybe they'd found Rose's meticulous rent book with my name inside. Yes, I realised, that must be it. Whatever the reason, I was neatly buttonholed in place. There was no way out of this.

'That's true,' I stuttered eventually, realising I had been silent for too long. 'But I really don't want to get involved, thank you.'

'Just a quick chat,' the officer said, with his foot already over the doorway.

At that moment, Jess came toddling out of the living room and tugged at my hand.

'Mammy,' she lisped. 'I'm hungry.'

Her innocence was the very antithesis of the Wests' evil. She was a tiny sunbeam, bursting through the darkest of clouds. My instinct was to run from this as far as I could.

'I'm really sorry, I don't want my children mixed up in this,' I stammered. 'I can't help you.'

The officer smiled. 'I understand that,' he said. 'But I just have one question, and you could be very helpful for the investigation.'

Shirley's face loomed large in my mind's eye. I looked at Jess, then pictured Shirley again and I was torn. My children were more important to me than anyone. But I owed it to Shirley. I could not fail her a second time. I knew what I had to do.

'One question,' the officer said again.

'Yes, OK,' I agreed, inviting him inside. 'How did you know I was there? Was I on the electoral roll?'

'Oh no,' he replied. 'We made door-to-door enquiries in Gloucester and your younger brother told us you lived there with your sister.'

Silently, I castigated my brother. He had dropped me right in the middle of the very mess I had been desperate to avoid. If I'd known there was nothing official linking me to Cromwell Street, I could have denied it, sent the officer away and said it was a mistake. It was wrong, I know. But I just didn't feel strong enough for this. My secrets were in a locked box, in a vault so deep it would cause me extreme pain even to locate it. And smashing open the lock might just smash me to pieces, too. The officer showed me a selection of photos of young women and asked me to pick out anyone I recognised.

191

'Yes, Shirley Robinson.' I nodded, pointing to Shirley's photo. 'I knew her. None of the others.'

'Do you know what relationship she had with Fred West?'

I nodded again. 'When I first moved in, Fred introduced Shirley as his lover, after pointing out his wife, Rose. I thought it was a silly fib back then. He seemed like a bit of a joker.'

The officer raised an eyebrow before packing away the photos and standing up.

'You've been so helpful,' he said. 'Can you please give me a recent photo of yourself and then I'll leave you in peace.'

I didn't ask why he needed the photo; I just did as he said, hoping he would leave. And as I closed the door behind him, I let out a long sigh of relief. I thought that was the end of it. I made Jess some toast and tried to put the visit out of my head.

But a few days later my phone rang, and I was told an officer was on his way to see me. This time, it was a different man, fair-haired and in a smart suit. He carried a briefcase.

'I'm really sorry but I want nothing to do with this,' I said as he settled himself onto the sofa.

'You will have to come to court,' he replied.

'No!' I said, my sharp voice betraying my panic. 'No, I can't.'

'You will be subpoenaed,' he explained. 'It means you will be forced to come. You have no choice.'

My eyes welled with tears. It sounded so selfish, not wanting to be involved. I understood that. So many young girls had died, and it was my duty to help the police. But at that time, I just did not feel able. Like a pot, filled to the brim with precious liquid, one more nudge would spill the lot. And everything would be lost. I could not risk that. I had to think of my children.

'Look,' the officer said, putting his pen down. 'I only need you to repeat that one sentence that you told my colleague. We require nothing else of you. But that single sentence will help us to get justice for Shirley. Do you think you could manage that?'

Again, I felt I was in the middle of a tug of war, Shirley pulling on one side, my children on the other. I owed it to them to stay out of this. I owed it to Shirley to tell the truth. To do the right thing.

'Just one sentence,' I agreed.

In a small voice, I repeated exactly what Fred had told me, and the officer wrote it down.

'You have been a tremendous help,' he said. 'We'll be in touch when you need to come to court.'

He did not ask if I had been sexually assaulted or abused by Fred West, or whether Rose had made advances towards me. He didn't ask me anything else at all. And I was glad he didn't, because I did not want to tell him. I wanted instead to bury those memories as deeply as I could, as deeply as if they were buried in the Cromwell Street garden. After the officer left, I sank onto a kitchen chair and my head dropped into my hands. The thought of testifying in court, with everyone watching and listening, was so frightening. I really wasn't sure I could do it.

I was all fingers and thumbs as I tried to button my smart jacket in front of the mirror.

'Is this OK, do you think?' I anxiously asked my friend Kelly.

I hadn't wanted to buy a new suit for the trial. It seemed distasteful, somehow, splashing out on new clothes to give evidence about Shirley's murder. And I couldn't afford any, either. But now that the day had arrived, an overcast October morning where the sky was the same gloomy grey colour as the land, I was having second thoughts. In my black jacket, black T-shirt and jeans, I felt hopelessly underdressed and underprepared, with all my misgivings diverted towards my outfit.

Kelly smiled. 'Kathy, you look fine,' she said. 'Stop worrying. You're going to be OK.'

We had arranged to meet liaison officers at a former police station outside the city centre, and they would take us to court. Kelly had offered to drive the first part of the journey and then come with me to court for support.

'You'll be all right, I promise,' she said again, as we waited at traffic lights.

But I felt so nervous and jittery, an itchy blush creeping along my collar as we drove. I was so worried about giving evidence. And the threat of having a seizure, in the witness box, hung over me like a black cloud. I hadn't even told the police about my fits. I hadn't told them anything, beyond that one statement from Fred. When we arrived at the meeting point, we were transferred into a large people carrier with blacked-out windows. Arriving at Winchester Crown Court, I heard the crowd even before I saw them.

'We're going to take you in the side entrance, but there's press outside every door,' warned one of the officers.

She handed me a blanket and I looked at it in confusion.

'For your head,' she explained. 'So you're not on the front page of tomorrow's papers.'

'I'll just use my jacket, thank you,' I said, my nerves shooting up another notch.

She was right to be concerned. The moment the car doors opened, there was a blaze of white light, cameras pushed right into my face, lenses poking under my makeshift hood. We were shoved and buffeted about, my feet nearly leaving the ground in the scrum. I might as well have been a scrap of litter in the wind. The reporters shouted a string of Christian names, and I realised they didn't know who I was, and were waiting for me to react to a name to identify myself.

'Don't say a word,' muttered the liaison officer behind me. 'Just keep moving.'

Inside the court building, I sat on the nearest chair I could find, my legs jelly-like and unable to hold me up any longer. As I got my breath back, I was ushered into a witness room and offered tea and digestives while I waited to be called. I both hoped and dreaded to hear my name. I wanted it over with quickly, but I also wanted it never to happen.

One hour on, I found myself standing in the witness box. This was my first ever time inside a court, and it was packed. The public gallery was jammed with onlookers. The press members were squashed in, more bodies than seats. There were high-brow lawyers and solicitors and clerks, and of course the judge. I did not have the confidence to look any of them in the eye. Dread swept through me. What if I had a seizure here, right in front of all these strangers? The humiliation did not bear thinking about. It was a vicious circle, of course. The more I worried, the more likely I was to have a seizure.

Stop it, Kathy, I said to myself firmly. *Just stop it.*

As I dared to raise my head, my stomach plunged as I saw Rose, directly in my eyeline.

Does she remember me? I wondered.

I had doubtless changed so much, and she had too. She looked much older and, although she had never been slim, she seemed heavier. Though her expression did not alter, she flicked her trademark sideways glance, contemptuous and superior, from under heavy eyelids. In that moment I was back at Cromwell Street, standing in the doorway of the living room, my legs quivering, just as they were now. Ambushed by a memory of Rose, legs akimbo in her see-through nightie, I shook my head a little, as though I had a nasty bug in my ear. Which, in a way, I did.

The prosecution barrister got to his feet and asked, 'Were you a lodger at Cromwell Street?'

'I was,' I replied timidly.

'Can you tell me about your arrival there?' he asked.

I started to speak, but I couldn't hear my own voice because my blood was rushing so loudly in my ears. I might as well have been standing at the side of a busy motorway.

'My sister and I left home,' I explained. 'We'd heard there were rooms at Cromwell Street and so we knocked on the door and Fred West answered. He showed us into their living area and he introduced us to his family.'

'And what did he say?' the barrister asked.

I felt so brittle and vulnerable, like a child on a stage, forced against her will to take part in a hideous play.

'He said' – I took a deep breath, for I now understood how significant this was –'"This is my wife, Rose, and this is my lover, Shirley." And he pointed at Shirley Robinson.'

There was a heartbeat of stunned silence in the court followed by frantic rustling and movement as most of the reporters scrambled out of their seats and out of the door. There was a general murmur of surprise from the public gallery, but Rose remained completely impassive, though I imagined she must have been bracing herself for many more revelations from me.

Fortunately for her, my secrets were interred inside me, set in cement, and I didn't know how to get them out.

'Why did all those reporters leave?' I asked, as I was shown back out into the corridor. 'Did I say something wrong?'

'Oh no,' replied the court usher. 'You just gave them their next headline. They were all rushing out to ring their editors and file their copy.'

Dizzy with a curious mixture of relief and anxiety, I was glad it was done but shaken by the resurfacing memories of that first day. Knocking on the door that afternoon had been the start of it all. I had become entangled in the Wests' lives, trapped in their peculiar and poisonous brand of evil. It was like being wrapped in barbed wire. Each time I tried to escape, the sharp points ripped at my skin and held me back. And they were holding me tight, even now. Back in the witness room, I was glad of a biscuit and a cup of tea to steady my nerves.

'Are you OK?' Kelly asked. 'You were shaking as you gave evidence, Kathy, I could see it. You reminded me of one of those nodding dogs, you looked so nervous.'

'I was,' I admitted. 'I'm glad it's over.'

As we sat, quietly sipping our tea, a young woman barged through the door, marched over, and said to me: 'You weren't at Cromwell Street! I know you weren't! I don't remember you!'

Wearily, I lifted my head to look at her.

'I really wish I hadn't been,' I replied, rattled, as two security staff came to lead her away.

I had no idea who she was – possibly a lodger or a friend of the Wests. Or maybe she was just a hanger-on who'd never even set foot in the house. It was entirely feasible she had lived at Cromwell Street without meeting me – I had lodged there for less than two years. Yet it was shocking that she would turn on me so viciously. It was yet another depressing lesson: in tragedy when you hope for the best from people, you will often see them at their worst. She had attacked the very people who needed her support.

'I can't breathe in here,' I said to the police officer, after she had gone. 'I need to get out. I need to get home.'

26

Exhausted by the stress of the court case, I got into my nightclothes at the same time as the children and was just about to go to bed when there was a knock at the front door. I answered and realised my mistake immediately. A young man, with a note pad and pen in his hand, smiled confidently underneath the glow of the streetlamp.

'I believe you were giving evidence in court earlier,' he said. 'Just a few quotes, if you don't mind, Miss Ryan? And maybe a photo?' He patted a brown camera bag over his shoulder and then flipped the top off his pen. 'Can I come inside?' he ventured. 'We could have a proper chat.'

Wordlessly, I slammed the door shut and locked it, then sank to the carpet and burst into tears. This was exactly what I had been dreading. I waited until I was sure he had gone and then I ran around the house, checking all the windows, closing the curtains and switching off the lights. The next morning, I kept the children home from school and nursery. I had already booked a few days off work, unsure how long I'd be needed in court. We hunkered down in the living room, playing board games and eating toast. When Jane called round, mid-afternoon, I ushered her inside quickly before bolting the door.

'Why are your curtains closed?' she asked. 'Are you ill?'

'No,' I said nervously. 'Not exactly. But I've had a reporter round and I'm terrified of anyone knowing I'm at home. I just can't face it, Jane. I'm not ready for all this.'

She frowned. 'You might not like this then,' she said, handing me a copy of our local newspaper. 'But it's best that you see it before someone else shows you.'

The headline seemed to leap at me from the front page: 'my wife, my lover' – house of horror lodger's testimony against evil Wests.

And inside, to my alarm, there was a sketch of me, drawn as I was giving evidence.

'On the bright side, it looks nothing like you,' Jane smiled. 'Nobody would recognise you at all!'

She was right, it was a poor likeness. But I was mortified to see my name and my words in print. Now, everyone would know. Everyone would judge me. Everyone would blame me.

'I don't understand why you feel so afraid,' Jane said gently. 'Nobody will judge you or blame you. They will have so much sympathy for you, living there as you did.'

I couldn't begin to explain it to her.

'I'm not leaving the house,' I vowed. 'I can't do it. I really can't.'

Jane offered to call round the next day, bringing with her fresh milk and bread and a copy of the newspaper. I didn't want to read it but the reports from the trial were impossible to ignore. If

I switched off the TV, they came on the radio, or the headlines screamed from every newspaper. If the initial discoveries of the bodies had been about who and where, then the trial focused on how, why and when. And this was every bit as ghastly, if not worse. For the prosecution, Brian Leveson presented Fred and Rose West as sadistic and sex-obsessed murderers and spoke of their sexual depravity. He revealed many of the victims had suffered horrendous sexual violence in their final moments of life and claimed they had been murdered to fulfil the sexual fantasies of the couple. The court was also told they had a previous conviction for indecent assault and assault against a young woman they had targeted in the early 1970s. I understood better than most people about Fred and Rose's perversions, yet this was grim, stomach-churning reading. Once again, I felt Fred's hands squeezing my bottom, his foul breath wafting in my face. Those same hands had ended so many lives.

It could have been you, a voice whispered in my ear.

It should have been you, said another coldly.

The prosecution witnesses included Cromwell Street lodgers, like me. There were also relatives of the victims, members of Rose's family, former lovers of the couple, former neighbours and acquaintances, and surviving victims, including Fred's daughter from his first marriage, Anne Marie West. For the defence, Dick Ferguson tried to discredit the prosecution witnesses as being motivated either by spite or by money. Neither allegation was relevant to me. I hadn't even wanted to give evidence. But I read the testimony of one survivor, herself a victim of their abuse, who said: 'I only want to get justice for the girls who didn't make it. I feel like it was my fault.'

Her words struck a chord deep within me; they could have

been mine. I remembered distinctly the young students who used to wait at Fred's car for a lift into town. I had thought – we had all thought – he was doing them a great favour. Now, I wondered what price they had paid. I was tormented too by flashbacks to the seizures I had in my bedroom at Cromwell Street. I'd thought it far-fetched to worry Fred might have assaulted me while I was unconscious. Now I had to accept the suggestion was entirely plausible. I would never know exactly how I had suffered at his hands. And perhaps that was for the best.

In the months after the bodies had been discovered, I thought a lot about Fred and Rose, and the lethal cocktail they had become together, bonded by their evil secrets. I wondered whether Britain's most dangerous couple's distinct types of depravity had merged to create a perfect storm where serial killers would flourish. Would they, I questioned, have become killers if they had never met?

My theories were pulled apart by the evidence at the trial, for it was revealed that Fred was already a killer when he met Rose, having murdered his teenage lover and later his first wife. I was also stunned to learn that in 1965 he had hit and killed a small boy while driving an ice-cream van. The death was an accident but the parallels with my own father and his ice-cream van were startling. As with his DIY obsession, Fred seemed to have so many traits with which I had identified and that had made me feel safe. The chasm between his reality and his lies could not have been greater. The newspapers also revealed that Fred had previously worked in an abattoir, developing skills that would serve him well in later life.

The prosecution explained that Fred and Rose had met at a

bus stop in early 1969, when Fred was twenty-seven and Rose just fifteen. By this time, Fred was already separated from his first wife, Catherine Costello, and he had a daughter Anne Marie and a stepdaughter Charmaine. Fred and Rose began a relationship, which her family disapproved of, and she became a full-time nanny to his two children. Her family made complaints to the authorities and, because Rose was still a child, she was placed in a home for wayward teenagers. Fred was later jailed for theft and non-payment of fines. But the couple were determined to be together and, by the following year, Rose was pregnant with their first child, Heather. They moved into a home on Midland Road in Gloucester, but Fred was again sent to prison for theft, leaving Rose, at the age of seventeen, to care for the three girls. Neighbours and family members reported that the children suffered unimaginable cruelty through physical and mental abuse. One witness claimed she visited the Wests to find Charmaine completely naked, gagged and bound on a chair, with Rose standing alongside her ominously holding a wooden spoon. The prosecution claimed that Rose had murdered Charmaine, aged eight, just days before her father was due for release from prison. Rose explained Charmaine's disappearance by claiming that she had gone to live with her mother, Fred's first wife, Catherine (also known as Rena). Fred backed up this story when he came home from prison. According to reports, Charmaine's body was initially stored in the coal cellar until Fred was released, after which he buried it in the garden, close to the back door. A post-mortem later indicated that the body had been sliced off at the hip. Several bones, including those of fingers, toes, wrists and ankles, were missing. This was a pattern found in all of the victims who were exhumed. Dismembered bodies were, the prosecution explained, easier to bury, but police believed Fred had, in an aggressive display of control, taken the missing body parts as keepsakes or trophies. He had buried the bodies in and around his home to maintain power over them. Being so close by, they could never escape him. Fatally, he failed to consider that neither could he escape them.

At the end of 1971, it was believed Rena had visited Fred and Rose, demanding to see her children, and this was the last time she was seen alive. The prosecution alleged that Rena was murdered in the back of Fred's Ford Popular car before being dismembered and buried in a field. In January 1972, just weeks after this brutal murder, Fred and Rose were married at Gloucester Register Office. That same year, Rose fell pregnant with their second child and they moved to 25 Cromwell Street, renting from the council initially before buying the property outright for £7,000. To fund his purchase, Fred, described in court as a builder, converted some of the upstairs rooms into bedsits and the couple began taking in lodgers. Rose meanwhile gave birth to a daughter, Mae June. Shortly afterwards, the court heard, she began to work as a prostitute, operating from an upstairs room at Cromwell Street and advertising her services, for both men and women, in a local magazine. She used a false name, 'Mandy', and had her own doorbell and a red light to indicate when she was busy. Rose carried the key for her room around her neck, an image I easily recalled. She was, according to the press, in charge of all money in the house, and I remembered in a flash how we had been ordered to pay our weekly rent directly to her. The reports claimed that much of her earnings from prostitution were spent on DIY and home improvements, a sick euphemism, I presumed, for burying the bodies.

It was so far-fetched, I would never have believed it, yet I knew it was true because I had been there. Suddenly, many of the riddles at Cromwell Street started to make sense. Each new piece of information slotted perfectly into the gaps that had troubled me during my time there. Each memory was now infused with new and unpalatable horror. I remembered the second doorbell only too well, and my timely escape from Fred and Rose when it rang. I now knew Rose had a client waiting that day. I remembered the red light, too, because Deirdre and I had joked in our innocence that they were planning a disco. And though I'd often heard the name 'Mandy' I presumed she was Rose's friend. I had no idea it was her twisted alter ego. I had been pitifully and cruelly conned. We all had.

In one newspaper report, prosecutors described a series of peepholes in Rose's bedroom through which she and Fred would watch each other having sex with other people.

'The peepholes!' I gasped, throwing down the newspaper. 'We had those in our room, too!'

While Deirdre and I had speculated on the identity of our spy, we had never for a moment thought it might be a woman. Reading the daily press reports, I was almost sick with disgust and disbelief. The papers revealed Fred and Rose regularly indulged in sadistic sexual activity, including bondage and extreme violence. They collected a number of restraining devices, magazines and photographs, as well as videos of bestiality and paedophilia. They also produced their own pornographic movies. Again, the revelations sent a shudder of recognition through me. I remembered the dirty film Rose had been watching when she invited me into her living room. I recalled Fred trying to coerce me into watching films with them. Then, as before, I'd had yet another lucky escape. It now seemed as though I would have been expected to take part in the films, as well as watching them.

By 1983, Rose had given birth to eight children, at least three of whom it was thought had been fathered by her clients. The children, reports claimed, were regularly beaten. Between 1972 and 1992 they were admitted to A&E thirty-one times, with each injury explained away as a domestic accident. Sickeningly, some of the children were subjected to horrific sexual abuse and rape and forced into prostitution. In anguish, I remembered the odd absence of children for long periods of time, especially at Christmas. It made sense now.

'How did we not know?' I sobbed, as I read the newspaper in disbelief. 'How?'

But I was able to answer my own question. Through bitter experience, I knew that abused children learn to hide their trauma expertly, especially if they are being coerced and threatened. Or if they feel they will not be believed. In August 1992, Fred was arrested after being accused of raping his daughter three times and Rose was arrested for child cruelty. But the following year the case was dropped when their daughter withdrew her statement. As a result of the complaint, the younger West children were finally removed from their parents and taken to live in foster homes. It was this that sparked the police investigation. While in care, the children told social workers about a 'family joke': for years they were told, 'If you're naughty, you'll end up like Heather, under the patio in the back garden.' Concerned welfare workers realised Heather had not been seen since 1987 and they alerted police, who started to dig in the Wests' garden. The so-called family joke turned out to be yet more macabre in reality as the couple's horrific secrets were at last exposed. The cellar at Cromwell Street, originally and ironically a playroom, had been turned into a demonic torture chamber where victims were raped, battered, murdered and buried beneath the floor. When they ran out of space, the Wests began burying victims in the garden instead.

27

After giving my evidence, I did not return to the courts. But I followed the daily reports, as everyone else did, not because I wanted to but because there was no escaping them. What angered me most about the press coverage was the way it focused so intensely on Fred and Rose West and much less on the poor girls who had died. Fred was stealing centre stage from his victims, even in death, playing the clown and getting away with it. He demanded, albeit posthumously, to be the centre of attention. So, when the victims were listed in the local paper, in order of their passing, I braced myself to read about them. There were a thousand invisible threads connecting me to each poor soul, and I wanted to remember them not as numbers but as people.

Fred's first known victim was Ann McFall, aged eighteen, who in 1966 had moved from her home in Scotland to Gloucestershire, where she took a job as a nanny to Fred's children from his marriage to Catherine Costello. Ann became

Fred's lover when his wife was not about, and she became pregnant with his child. In May 1967, when she was eight months pregnant, she disappeared. Her remains, and those of her unborn child, were discovered in a field in Kempley, Gloucestershire.

Catherine, or Rena, Costello, Fred's first wife, was Scottish too. She had married Fred in 1962 when she was already pregnant with someone else's child. In 1963, she gave birth to a daughter, Charmaine. The following year, the couple had a daughter together, Anne Marie. Catherine disappeared aged twenty-six and her remains were found buried in a field close to where Ann McFall was discovered.

Fred and Rose were jointly accused of murdering ten women together, the first and youngest of whom was Fred's eight-year-old stepdaughter, Charmaine.

Lynda Gough lived and worked in Gloucester and became friendly with the lodgers who lived at 25 Cromwell Street. She was reported missing by her family in April 1973 and her remains were found in a garage, converted into a bathroom, at Cromwell Street.

Carole Ann Cooper was from Luton and was living in a children's home when she disappeared in November 1973. She was reported missing by her grandmother after vanishing on her way home from a night out. Her body was found buried in the cellar at Cromwell Street and police believed she had been abducted by the Wests while hitchhiking.

Lucy Partington was twenty-one years old and studying at Exeter University when, in December 1973, she came home to Gloucester for Christmas. She vanished two days later after visiting a friend and her mother reported her missing. Police believed she had been picked up by the Wests as she waited for her bus home. Her remains were discovered under the cellar floor at Cromwell Street.

Therese Siegenthaler was born in Switzerland and, at twenty-one, was a secretarial student in London. Over Easter 1974, she set out to hitchhike to Ireland to visit a friend but never arrived. It was thought she had been picked up by Fred and Rose West on her journey. She, too, was found under the floor of the cellar.

Shirley Hubbard was fifteen years old and the youngest victim to be found at Cromwell Street. She was also known as Shirley Lloyd and Shirley Owen. Born in Birmingham, she was taken into care as a small child. In November 1974, she was working in Debenhams in Worcester and disappeared on her way home from work. Her remains were discovered under the cellar floor at the Wests' home.

Juanita Mott was from Gloucester but had left the city for work. In 1975, she was travelling back to attend a friend's wedding, when she vanished. Her remains were later found in the cellar of 25 Cromwell Street.

Shirley Anne Robinson was born in Leicestershire and had lived in Germany and the West Midlands. Fred had been assigned an appropriate adult during police interviews because of learning difficulties and there were reports that, before his suicide, he had admitted to the appropriate adult how Rose had murdered Shirley and assisted in her dismemberment, removing the foetus from her womb in the process. Shirley's murder was different from the others since she was apparently killed because of her pregnancy and not for sexual kicks. The press reported she was Fred's lover and, like Ann McFall, was eight months pregnant with his child when she disappeared in May 1978.

She and her unborn child were found buried in the garden of Cromwell Street.

Reading Shirley's brief obituary was hardest of all. I remembered the way Rose had nudged her and glared at her in the kitchen. The tension between them, as the months passed, had stretched tight like elastic. And in those weeks before her murder, Shirley had moved out of the bedroom she shared with Fred. Perhaps Rose was jealous and resentful, especially if she heard Shirley's constant assurances that she and Fred would raise their baby together. Maybe Shirley was murdered because she was a threat. And Fred's lie about her moving to Germany was either a lucky coincidence or it was based on prior research, because reports claimed Shirley had lived there in the past. Her baby, only a month from the due date, would likely have survived if she had given birth early. For me, her baby was another victim. As was Ann McFall's baby. They had no voice, nobody to call for justice on their behalf. And so they were forgotten.

Alison Chambers was only sixteen when she disappeared. Born in Germany, she later moved to Swansea and was then moved to a children's home in Gloucester. She was a regular visitor to 25 Cromwell Street and it was reported she had moved in there early in 1979. Shortly before her seventeenth birthday in August that year, she vanished. Her remains were found in the garden at 25 Cromwell Street.

The final known victim of Fred and Rose West was, tragically, their eldest child, Heather West. She was murdered in 1987 at the age of sixteen, shortly after finishing her GCSEs. Police believed she was killed after threatening to speak to the authorities about the abuse she and her siblings were suffering at the hands of their parents. The Wests told people she had left home to work at a holiday village in Devon but her remains were discovered buried under the patio at Cromwell Street. Though she was the last victim, she was the first to be discovered.

The police images of the twelve victims flickered on and off in my brain like dying candles. I tortured myself with thoughts of their pain and terror, of their final moments. I recalled only too well the revolting feel of Fred's damp hands on my skin. For these poor girls, this was their last ever memory. All through my life, I had disconnected myself from my trauma. Strangely dislocated and distant, I had almost been able to pretend it hadn't happened as the years passed. But now, on behalf of these tragic girls, I embraced every detail of their suffering. On their part, my heart wept and my soul bled. And yet, if this was my punishment, it still was not enough. It could never be enough.

Ever since her arrest, Rose had pleaded not guilty and at the trial she insisted on giving evidence in her own defence. She was described in newspaper reports as having dramatic mood swings – sometimes smiling, even strangely humorous, but other days mournful and weeping. Memories reared up before me: Rose simpering and silly, speaking in her little-girl voice. Rose screaming and swearing, spitting with anger. Yes, I knew all about those mood swings.

The reports said that she was a mother of ten children, including two stepchildren. I was struck again by the odd absence of children in Cromwell Street. I had often wondered where they all were, but I understood now how and why they had been hidden away. And not for the first time, cold horror trickled through my veins as I thought about Rose as a mother.

I still carried my own scars after the termination and I understood something of the pain and anguish of losing a baby. How
could any mother hurt her own child? Rose had murdered her
own child and her stepchild. And she had wickedly, unfor-
givably, robbed other mothers of their children, too. I could
not help thinking of that first day at Cromwell Street and the
sick charade they had presented – Mum, Dad and children.
A normal family. Fred's welcome and his silly jokes had put
me at ease, when I should have been running as fast and as far
away as I could.

The very least Rose could have done – the one, small droplet
of comfort for her victims' families – would have been to admit
her guilt. But she did not. All through the trial, she stuck like
glue to her wicked lies. The court heard tapes of interviews with
Fred in which he claimed he was the sole killer. He had handed
a note to the interview team that said, 'I have not and still
cannot tell you the whole truth ... from the very first day of this
enquiry my main concern has been to protect another person
or persons.' Fred frequently changed his story and eventually
denied being involved in any of the murders. The prosecution's
case was that the couple had formed a pact whereby Fred would
take full responsibility for all the murders.

Almost six weeks on, six weeks of gut-wrenching revelations,
the jury retired to consider their verdicts. Sick with anticipation,
I was on tenterhooks, waiting for them to come back in. The
trial eclipsed all else. I was at the centre of this, yet it was the
last place I wanted to be. I was certain in my heart that Rose
was guilty, but I worried she might somehow slither free. After
all, she and Fred had got away with murder for twenty years.

On 21 November 1995, the jury returned guilty verdicts on

213

three of the murders, with seven left to come. The following evening, as I drove home from work, the news came on the radio.

'Rosemary West, Britain's most prolific female serial killer, has been convicted of all ten murders, following some of the most disturbing evidence ever heard in a court of law.'

The relief hit me like a tidal wave and, brimming with emotion, I had to pull over to the side of the road.

'At last,' I said, with a heavy sigh. 'At last.'

Resting my head on the steering wheel, the tears fell fast. My heart was breaking for each and every girl, but especially for Shirley, my lost friend.

'I'm sorry,' I whispered. 'I wish I could have saved you.'

And there it was again – the guilt, creeping like poison ivy under my skin. Behind closed eyes, I saw the rosy apple, the bottle-green trousers, the cold, hard penny. Ever since that day, I had spent my life taking the blame and apologising. Would it never end?

Rose West was sentenced to life imprisonment at HMP Low Newton in County Durham, alongside Myra Hindley and other violent female offenders. Justice Charles Mantell told her she should never be released.

To the jurors he said: 'You will never have had a more important job to do in your life – I am aware of the great stress it must have placed you under. You deserve my thanks and the country's for the part you have played.'

By the time I arrived home, Rose's solicitor was on the TV news, informing reporters that she would be appealing the verdict, claiming negative media coverage had prejudiced the trial. Rose West's mugshot flashed onto the screen and I caught my breath. It had captured her perfectly and I recognised all too well that look, somewhere between a smirk and a glare, succinctly conveying how bored she was and how she was better than everyone else. Even now, guilty of ten horrific murders, she showed no remorse, no shame. At a later police press conference, officers admitted Fred had confessed to associates that he had killed more than twelve victims. He had boasted, in years gone by, of killing hundreds. The true figure would never be known. The missing body parts of his known victims, mainly kneecaps and fingers, had never been found. Police revealed that, as a result of their inquiries, 110 missing people were found safe and well, which was a crumb of comfort in the very bleakest of cases. A staggering number of officers and civilian staff had worked on the investigation and, at its peak in March 1994, there were eighty-four officers involved with the inquiry. The investigation took the police over budget by £772,604. All officers had been offered counselling.

There were questions too about how and why Fred and Rose West had been able to get away with their crimes over a twenty-year period, in particular against those victims who were in the care of the authorities. There was criticism of the way the abuse of the Wests' own children had been missed. But it was explained that, in the 1970s, as I knew to my cost, there was little or no communication between agencies such as police, teachers, hospitals and social services. Information was not shared and cases were not linked in the same way that they are now. Only six of the twelve victims had been reported missing to police. Again, I recalled my mother's visits to Cromwell Street and heard her voice as she asked for Deirdre and me. Her presence, however fleeting, had kept me safe. Despite the distance and the differences between us, I felt a well of gratitude. I called to thank her.

'I think those visits, on your way to Linbar's, are the reason I'm still here today,' I told her.

'You've been lucky,' she agreed.

And though she knew nothing of Fred and Rose's behaviour towards me, I knew she was right. I was, at least, alive.

28

For days after the conclusion of the trial, I locked myself away at home. Once again, I was a prisoner of four walls. Escaping my bedroom in Cromwell Street, I'd thought I was running towards the fresh air of freedom. Yet here I was, captive again, with my secrets hidden away with me. The problem was, I could not hide from myself. After the sentencing, I heard nothing more from the police. There was no follow-up call, no support or advice. But, of course, they had no inkling of what I had been through at Cromwell Street. And so I was in limbo, suspended in a strange state, a little like the day after a funeral. It was hard to know how to behave and how to return to normal life, whatever that was. Deirdre coped differently and she accepted an offer to appear on a television talk show to discuss her time at Cromwell Street.

'Why don't you come on too?' she asked. 'It would do you good, Kathy. We have nothing to be ashamed of. You had it so much worse than I did.'

But I shuddered at the suggestion. There was no way I could share my trauma with the world. I could not even face going out to the shops. John's school was nearby, and he walked to and from with his friends, so I had no need to leave the house for the school run. I kept Jess off school and, though I could not afford it, I stayed off work too. Jane was a good friend, calling round most days with provisions. She was patient and understanding.

But one afternoon, she marched in, threw open the curtains, and said: 'Enough is enough, Kathy! You can't carry on like this.'

Without waiting for my reply, she helped Jess into her coat and shoes and threw me my coat.

'Come on,' she said. 'We're going out.'

'I can't,' I protested but Jane was already leading me, kindly but firmly, towards the front door. Looking out into the street was like looking out over a precipice. My mind was in freefall, my stomach was rolling.

'Nobody will say a word to you,' Jane promised. 'Don't worry. People are very sympathetic towards you, Kathy. They understand how brave you were, testifying against the Wests.'

I didn't believe her. I didn't deserve anyone's sympathy. But she was right – nobody said a thing to me. Yet as we walked down the high street to the local Co-op, I felt their stares drilling through the back of my head, the faint traces of their gossip trailing in my wake. Tainted by association, I felt branded and blamed. And the guilt – the draining, scorching guilt – dragged along with me, every step of the way along the street.

They will blame me, I said to myself. *They will all blame me. I could have saved those poor girls.*

My feelings made no sense and, on one level, I knew that. But regardless, they burrowed like parasites through my soul.

I let him do it. I let him get away.

The next day, Jane called round again, this time persuading me to walk to the chip shop with her.

'You've lost weight,' she told me. 'You need a good meal. My treat.'

I ordered a mince beef pie with chips and, to my surprise, I enjoyed every mouthful. Huddled outside on a bench, with the weak winter sunlight on my face, I realised she was right. I could not carry on like this for ever. I owed it to my children to take them out, to have fun, to live life. I needed my wages, too.

Slowly but surely, I began forcing myself to rejoin society, leaving the house for just a few moments at a time, before I was strong enough to return to work. Completing my first full week of shifts felt like a major achievement, and I knew I owed Jane a huge debt.

'Thank you,' I said. 'I couldn't have done this without you.'

'You've been through a lot, Kathy,' she said, squeezing my hand.

But even then, I could not confide in her about Cromwell Street. She knew only that I had been a lodger there and knew nothing of the abuse or the assaults. Jane was a true friend, though, and she did not push me further. My secrets remained hidden, buried far beneath the surface, inaccessible even to me.

In March 1996, I read in the news that Rose's application to appeal her convictions had been rejected. Then followed stories that she had become friendly with Myra Hindley. There were sick claims that Rose had commandeered a plush cell for herself, a better one than everyone else's. Another report described how she had been punched in the face by a fellow prisoner.

'West has got a fan club, she gets the most fan mail,' said the prisoner in question. 'She walks around the jail like she owns it.'

My blood boiled with resentment. Even after her conviction, even after the world had found out what she was and what she had done, she was still a hot topic of gossip. People could not get enough of her – to the point, if the report was to be believed, of sending her fan mail. It beggared belief and, as it had been so many times before, my trust in humanity was badly shaken. I could not imagine how hard it must have been for the families and friends of the victims, hearing about Rose's twisted exploits while their loved ones were so quickly forgotten.

Meanwhile, there was speculation locally that Fred had buried more bodies around Gloucester. There was even a petition in the local shop to excavate a cafe where a missing girl had worked. I could not bring myself even to read it. I felt there had been enough digging and enough heartbreak. Fred and Rose had been in the spotlight for far too long already and poking at the nest of snakes would only lead to more poisonous bites.

Later in 1996, I was in the supermarket when a headline on the news rack caught my eye:

House of horror to be demolished!

Wobbly with shock, I leaned on my shopping trolley and took a deep breath.

'Thank goodness,' I said out loud, not caring who heard me. 'Good riddance.'

Abandoning the rest of my shopping list, I bought a copy of the newspaper and read the article immediately. Gloucester City Council had announced that 25 Cromwell Street was to be demolished completely, along with a neighbouring building. The council had bought the Wests' home for £40,000, with cash from the sale benefitting the younger West children. The plan was to completely erase it from existence. I read that each brick would be removed one by one, before being crushed and mixed with other waste and poured into pre-prepared holes at a council recycling centre. The timber structures would be burned and all fittings melted down. The house, like its tragic occupants, was set to disappear completely.

'Good,' I said again.

My mind rushed back to images of the long kitchen, the narrow hallway, the chest of drawers I had used to keep Fred out of our bedroom, the scratchy green blanket, the dodgy plug sockets. And I saw again, vivid in colour and texture, that lonely bag of baby clothes. It had probably been disposed of long ago. If not, it was soon to be incinerated. Everything, the last speck of dust, the last chip of paint, would vanish. The city council had said that complete destruction was necessary because of the 'sensitive nature of the site' and, as the relief coursed through me, I could not have agreed more. I was certain this was the right thing to do. The house stood like a monument to evil, a reminder of all that was bad in the world. It had no place in Gloucester, or anywhere in the universe for that matter.

'They're knocking Cromwell Street down,' I told Jane, showing her the newspaper when I saw her that evening.

'Good riddance,' she said, repeating my sentiment.

I imagined so many people felt just the same. Over the next two weeks, the local paper carried pictures of the demolition work. The street itself was closed off and there was a police guard at the site to deter grisly souvenir hunters. One report revealed the fancy white sign – '25 Cromwell Street' – was at the centre of legal wrangling. The sign had been removed from the wall by police during the early searches because they feared it would attract ghoulish trophy hunters. Two years on, it remained locked away at a Gloucester police station, while law-yers argued over its future. Some members of the West family were apparently anxious to take ownership of it, while the police wanted it destroyed. I could not understand why anyone would want to own a piece of pure evil. But though I was saddened, I was not surprised. Ever since the first remains had been discov-ered, people had swarmed like wasps around Cromwell Street, eager to pick up anything connected to the tragedy. At the end of the demolition, a concrete cap was poured onto the area to seal it completely.

'I'd like to drive past,' I said to Jane. 'Check it's gone, for real.'

I hoped the confirmation might help me somehow – another small step forward. Jane drove us down to the dead end where the Wests' house had once been. She signalled to move over to their side of the road so she could park and we could get out. But I shook my head and shivered.

'I don't want to get out of the car, thank you,' I said. 'I couldn't stand on the spot where the house was. Not now that I know there were people buried underneath.'

A concrete path had been created down the side of where the house had stood, a short cut, away from the main road. But, for me, it would never be a walkway. It would always be a graveyard. Physically, this was the end for 25 Cromwell Street. I only wished it could be so effectively erased from our minds.

29

A few months after the trial, I moved house, desperate to leave behind the neighbours and friends who knew I'd been a lodger at Cromwell Street. I'd had no negativity from anyone – the criticism was all in my mind. But I hoped a new home might mean a new start. Once again, I was running away. But, once again, I could not outrun myself.

Our new place was on the Bristol Road, away from the city centre, away from Cromwell Street and all the reminders that had popped up, like boils, every time I left our old house. There was a pub opposite our new house, and I got part-time work as a chambermaid. The children settled in well, viewing the move as an adventure. We had a spare bedroom, and so I decided to sign up to a scheme to look after French exchange students. I liked having children around, and it was a way of earning a little extra. I also thought it would be a good experience for my own children, and they might even learn some French. Through the exchange company, I became friendly with a lady named Clara who lived down my street. One bright afternoon, she and I were having a coffee in her garden when a man popped his head over the fence.

'This is my neighbour, Mike Richards,' Clara said with a smile.

We chatted briefly and, later that evening, Clara called.

'Mike's just been round,' she said. 'He really likes you. I told him you were single. He wants your number. What do you think?'

'No thank you,' I said, without a moment's consideration. 'Nothing personal. But honestly, I'm happy on my own. I'm not really cut out for relationships.'

But the next time I was at Clara's, Mike just happened to call in to borrow something. And the week after that, he was standing in his garden when I arrived.

'Are you trying to set me up, by any chance?' I asked Clara, and she giggled.

'He's such a lovely man, Kathy,' she said. 'Just give him a chance. I think you'd be perfect for each other.'

Weeks later, worn down by Clara's persistence, Mike and I arranged to go for a drink. I took my brother and a friend along as chaperones. But I soon realised I didn't need them. Mike was quiet, kind and a real gentleman. He was tall, with lots of striking blonde hair, and I felt myself falling for him, even on that first date. He was the same age as me and seemed so dependable. We started seeing each other. I was waiting for a bombshell, for something to go drastically wrong, but it never did. Six months on, we moved in together. Mike had two children and he was a wonderful stepdad to John and Jess, raising them as his own. He was a hard worker and ran his own gardening business, and even in the winter months, when the ground was frozen hard, he insisted on going out to check on his elderly customers.

'Even when I can't dig the garden, I can make them a hot drink and maybe get them some shopping,' Mike said.

That was what I loved about him most. He had such a big heart. He was a DIY enthusiast, a disturbing thread that seemed to link all the major characters in my life. But, I told myself firmly, Mike was not like my father. And he was certainly nothing like Fred West. Though I was wary at first, I learned over time that DIY skills were not necessarily something to be suspicious of and I grew to appreciate Mike's skills around our home as he painted and decorated, plugged holes and fixed leaks.

'Good as new,' he'd say with his gentle smile.

Waving away my worries that I might not fit in, Mike took us away on our first foreign holidays, to Spain and later to Greece.

'Please don't book anywhere posh,' I said to him.

I really didn't feel I was the sort of person who deserved to go abroad. But Mike seemed to understand and I didn't need to explain.

'It's a basic apartment, I promise,' he said.

With him, nothing was a problem. His family welcomed me and my children as though they had known us for years. Mike's parents lived in Wales, and we'd often stay with them for the weekend. I became good friends with his sister, Jill. At last, I felt part of a loving, extended family. We were a unit – dependable, strong and happy.

Even so, it took me over a year to pluck up the courage to confide in Mike about my past. I had never told anyone what had happened to me at Cromwell Street. Even with Deirdre, I had glossed over the full facts of the attacks, believing it was pointless to upset her with the more invasive aspects of Fred's abuse. Perhaps part of that had been self-preservation – I had been too shell-shocked to acknowledge the truth myself. Certainly, my mother's reaction to my abuse had also shaped me. I felt I could not confide in anyone – I had tried it once and not been believed.

And now, as Mike held my hand and waited patiently, there were still details that stuck in my throat and which I kept back from him. I just could not say them out loud. Starting with that fateful day, the stolen apple and the bench outside the factory, I told him first of all about the caretaker.

'I kept on going back, for a penny,' I wept. 'I did it all in exchange for a strawberry sweet.'

Mike shook his head. 'You didn't *do* anything,' he insisted. 'You were just a little girl. He did it *to* you. You must see that.'

Next, I recounted the story of my grandad's abuse, remembering the single boiled potato he had presented to me as a reward.

'The fact that I was so pleased with the potato is somehow more shaming than the abuse itself,' I admitted. 'That's how little I valued myself.'

'You have nothing to be ashamed of,' Mike told me. 'Nothing at all.'

His eyes widened when I confided I had been a lodger at the Wests' house.

'I remember all the press coverage,' he said. 'It was dreadful.'

In between my tears, I explained how Fred West had groomed and groped me, day after day, for over a year.

'Fred used to chase me down the hallway and pin me against the wall to squeeze me,' I muttered, with my head in my hands. I couldn't bear to see Mike's reaction. 'Or he'd slap my bum when I bent over. Or he'd offer to show me his Thing.'

As I spoke, I chided myself for sounding so weak. Why hadn't I fought back more, why hadn't I kicked harder and yelled louder? Why didn't I move out after that first attack and sleep on the streets rather than stay under that roof? Why hadn't I gone to the police station and screamed until someone listened? Why hadn't I called social services or gone to hospital? Why didn't I report Shirley as a missing person? Why, why, why . . . ? Even now, after everything, the guilt itched and burned under my skin.

'I should have gone to the police,' I sobbed. 'It's my biggest regret. I don't know why I stayed quiet.'

And yet, deep down, I knew exactly why. Because I was not worthy. Because I had been made to wear urine-soaked clothes as a child. Because I had scraped chewing gum off the street to eat. Because I'd been forced to accept sweets in exchange for being sexually abused. Because Fred West and my grandad and the caretaker were popular and well liked and well respected. And because, all of my life, a lack of care and a lack of love meant that I had no self-belief, no sense of worth at all.

'It wouldn't have made any difference at all if you'd reported the Wests,' Mike said. 'You know that. People had reported him in the past, but he always wriggled out of it. People looked up to him. They wouldn't have believed you.

'Besides, you couldn't have known about the murders, let alone prevented them. Nobody could. If the police and social services didn't know what was going on, how on earth could you know? You were just a kid.'

I nodded dismally but I still could not shake the conviction that I was somehow responsible for Shirley's death. That it should have been me, and not her, buried in the back garden of

Cromwell Street. I was the one who got away, and I was paying for it, every moment of my life. The patina of shame clung to me as surely as if it had been painted onto my skin.

'You were just a kid,' Mike said again. 'I don't understand why you feel responsible.'

I didn't understand it, either. But that didn't change the way I felt. And I could not tell Mike about the more serious attacks, about Fred and Rose dragging me off the street, or Fred and Rose forcing me into their living room, or Fred assaulting me in my own bed as I slept. The images were raw and vivid in my mind as if they were happening at that moment. I wanted to tell Mike; I wanted to share my burden. But the words clogged in my mouth.

You are worthless, Kathy. You deserved everything you got.

Late in 1996, Mike and I were out for a drink in the local pub when he took my hand and said, 'Will you marry me, Kathy?'

My heart was bursting with love as I threw my arms around him. 'Yes! Yes, I will.'

I'd never felt surer of anyone or anything in my life. But even as we poured champagne and celebrated with the bar staff and the other customers, a small, mean voice whispered in my ear: *You don't deserve to be happy, Kathy. You don't deserve this.*

30

When Clara heard our wedding was booked for Valentine's Day 1997, she resumed the role of Cupid.

'I've called the TV news and they're sending cameras down to film your big day, because you're getting married on Valentine's. It's so romantic!' she announced.

'Oh, Clara!' I groaned, with a smile.

I didn't really want to be centre of attention, but I knew the kids would love being on telly. Mike and I were married at Gloucester Register Office in a beautiful ceremony. John gave me away and Jess was my bridesmaid. Afterwards, we smiled for the TV cameras and Mike gave a short interview.

'Congratulations, Mr and Mrs Richards!' everyone yelled as we left the register office.

I flushed with delight. Yet underneath my smiles, like a fast-running sewer, was the conviction that I was completely out of place here. I did not deserve the cameras or the well wishes. I did not deserve Mike, and I did not deserve happiness.

It should have been you, whispered a voice in my ear, as I threw my bouquet. It was a mocking, teasing voice. A voice with a thick West Country accent. A voice that sent a tremor down my spine.

For our honeymoon, Mike and I stayed at a Greek villa with an orange tree right outside. Each morning, Mike climbed the tree to pick two oranges for our breakfast and, as we sat in the sunshine, blissfully contented, I did my best to push away those dissenting voices that told me I had no right to be so. The good news kept coming, too, because after we arrived home, I discovered I was pregnant. It was a wonderful surprise and we were both thrilled. Everything went well and, as the weeks passed, I had insatiable cravings for cooked chicken. Sometimes, I'd buy two chickens at once from Asda, finishing one before I'd even arrived home. I couldn't get enough of it.

Our daughter, Hannah, was born that November, perfectly healthy and just as gorgeous as her big brother and sister. Jess adored her, treating her like a real-life doll. Each morning, she selected an outfit for her little sister and helped to wash and dress her. Seeing them all play together, I reminded myself how lucky I was. This was the type of childhood I'd longed for when I was small and had dreamed of creating for them. Mike and I worked hard to raise our family, and every penny we earned was for our children. We had no shortage of money or food or, most importantly, love. Yet, though cocooned in happiness, my self-esteem struggled. The abuse was like a permanent smudge, a smear of mud on a white dress that no amount of scrubbing would budge.

So when, one year, Mike suggested we have a holiday in a fancy hotel, I shook my head doubtfully.

'I really don't think that's my kind of place,' I said.

I could not bear to articulate it, but what I meant was: *I am not good enough to stay there. Nice hotels are for nice people. Not damaged people like me.*

My insecurities were also exposed in the way I raised the children – I was very overprotective. Though I was happy to invite their pals along for holidays and sleepovers with us, I did not encourage them to accept return invitations. I hated them being out of my sight, worried that they might fall prey to predators as I had. When Jess was eleven, she pleaded to be allowed to go on her first sleepover to a friend's house and, reluctantly, with Mike's support, I gave in.

'We'll devise a code,' I told her. 'I'll call the house at eight-thirty p.m. to say good night to you. If you say, "Yes, I'm fine, Mam", then I'll know you're in trouble and you need to come home immediately. I'll get straight in the car to collect you.'

Jess rolled her eyes but agreed to my terms, and it became our standard routine. Each time she stayed out overnight, I'd call at 8.30 p.m. on the dot, hoping never to hear the dreaded words: 'Yes, I'm fine, Mam.'

As an adult, Jess has travelled all over the world and often when she calls, from Hong Kong or Vietnam, I'll ask how she is and she'll reply: 'Yes, I'm fine, Mam,' in a deadpan voice, which sends us both into hysterics.

Slowly, I've learned to let my children go; it's part of being a parent. But when they were small, I found it so tough. My old uncertainties about people in authority resurfaced, too. I never had enough confidence to speak with police officers, teachers or doctors. I was in awe of them all, convinced they were more important and intelligent than me. On the bottom rung of life, blemished and broken, I was just a nobody.

At Hannah's parents' evenings, her teachers always enthused about how bright she was.

'With your consent, we'd like to put her in for a scholarship for a private secondary school,' they said. 'She's exceptionally clever.'

Inside, I was bursting with pride. But, on the outside, I could barely make eye contact with her form teacher. All I managed to mumble was: 'Well, she doesn't get that from me.'

Incredibly, Hannah passed the entrance exams with flying colours and was awarded the scholarship. There was great celebration in our house on her first day at her new school. But in the playground later that afternoon, I was swamped by an all-too familiar feeling of inferiority. The echoes of my past were like dusty cobwebs, brushing against my face, reminding me always that I would never be good enough. I had dressed up in my best blouse and trousers and a smart coat, hoping I wouldn't look too out of place. But listening to the other parents chatting, I wanted to crawl back into my car and hide. They all sounded so intelligent, so educated. When someone asked me the name of my daughter, I did my best to affect a posh accent, worried they would realise I was Irish. Yet I was not ashamed of being Irish. I was ashamed of being me.

'You're as good as anyone there,' Mike told me later. 'Don't let it bother you.'

And for the most part, I didn't. I worked hard to ensure that my self-doubt was contained within me and not transferred onto our children. They all thrived, and we enjoyed our busy home life so much that we decided to become foster carers. I had really enjoyed hosting the French exchange students years earlier, and I knew that, through foster care, I might really be able to make a difference to those children who needed it the most. We made an application and began the lengthy process of checks and assessments. But when the social worker asked about our backgrounds, I felt a drawbridge quickly lifting in my mind, as I shut myself off from the pain of the abuse of years gone by.

'My childhood wasn't all roses,' I said carefully.

The social worker smiled warmly. 'Well, whose is?' she replied, and moved on to the next question.

Our first foster placement, a teenage girl, arrived the following year. I enjoyed taking her shopping, cooking her favourite meals, encouraging her at school. It was as though the job was made for me. I loved bringing maternal warmth into a child's life, for I knew how desolate it felt to grow up without it. I never told our foster children about my own suffering, but my experiences were definitely valuable.

One day, I spotted a pattern of blood on a bedsheet and suspected our foster child, a troubled boy in his early teens, was self-harming. Checking his inner arms provided the confirmation I was dreading. I allowed him a day off school and made us both a cup of tea.

'I want to know what's going on with you,' I said.

'What would you know?' he snapped. 'You've no idea about kids like me.'

'Oh!' I replied, slapping my hands on my knees. 'You have no idea. Get yourself comfy if you want to hear my secrets. We could be here a while!'

I didn't tell him any details, of course. But I did manage to make him laugh. I gave him an elastic band, too, which we agreed he should ping every time he had the urge to self-harm.

We looked after one child who was transgender and struggling to find acceptance. Another child had Irish roots, and she loved watching *My Big Fat Gypsy Wedding* with me and chatting about home. One summer, after we'd booked a holiday to France, we were asked to look after a boy in his mid-teens for a few months. The fostering agency couldn't pay for him to come to France and advised us to leave him in respite care instead. But I could not bear to leave him behind.

'How is he supposed to trust me if I dump him and go off on holiday?' I asked.

Mike and I covered the cost of his holiday ourselves, and our foster son had a wonderful time. We stayed at an all-inclusive resort and he helped himself to four puddings with every meal. He was far too thin, and I was pleased he was eating so much. When we got home, the social worker called round for an update and, to my dismay, the boy told her we hadn't fed him at all in France. Open-mouthed, I showed the social worker countless photos of us all eating together, with his puddings lined up on the table. I was so upset about his lie that I was reduced to tears.

'Kathy, I know you're telling the truth,' said the social worker. 'This boy is so used to being rejected that he is pushing you away before you can push him away.'

The explanation tugged at my heart and I vowed to keep trying. But there was no quick fix. No cure. I knew that better than anyone.

Another child, who had been abused by her parents, was desperate to leave us and return home to them.

'I don't understand it,' Mike said, baffled. 'Why does she want to go back to someone who treated her so badly?'

'It's not so simple,' I replied, as images of the caretaker, my grandad and Fred West burst across my eyeline. 'When you're being abused, you feel like you deserve it. You keep going back for more because it's normal. It's all you know. And sometimes, if it's a family member, you love your abuser. It's possible to love someone who is destroying you.'

Surrounded by children who came and went, and who hopefully left our home happier and healthier, I was in my element. Friends joked that I was like the old lady who lived in a shoe. It was hard work, tiring, infuriating and often challenging. The agency had rules that all children had to be in by 10 p.m. and if they were late I had a duty to call the police. It was a big effort for me to pluck up courage to speak with a police officer, but I owed it to the children in my care. And after those first few calls, I grew in confidence. I enjoyed working with the local officers, keeping my charges safe. Right through the early hours, I'd doze in the living room, waiting for the sound of a police car outside bringing a lost chicken home to roost. Fostering was exhausting and nerve-racking but the rewards were amazing, and I felt I had found my calling.

But while the children were all doing well, Mike and I were slowly drifting apart. I was always busy doing school runs and drop-offs for football training and ballet class and chess club. In the evenings, my time was taken up with homework or spelling tests or art projects. And, if I ever found a spare minute, I had a never-ending pile of washing and ironing. Or I might walk the dog or sew on a PE name badge or shine school shoes. And I always, always, found time to clean. Cleaning was my therapy, just as it had been when I was small. Mike and I communicated less and less about each other and more and more about the children:

Can you pick up from the after-school club and take them swimming?

Any chance you could help Hannah make a carboard castle for history?

And John has a puncture on his bike – can you look at it?

We were a great team, but there was no longer any fun or affection between us. Intimacy was still a struggle for me. Revolting images of the Thing haunted me every time Mike and I were in bed. Sometimes, those moments of closeness triggered nausea and sickness and, more than once, I suffered a seizure. I hated that the abuse was seeping, like damp, into every corner of my life. But I didn't know how to stop it. Memories of the past reached out to clutch at me, desperate ghosts with their sharp fingernails digging under my skin.

Mike and I had been fostering for five years when, resigned and unhappy, I suggested we should separate.

'There doesn't seem to be much point any more,' he agreed sadly.

He moved out and I stayed in our family home, with Hannah, aged fifteen, and our foster children. John, aged twenty-nine, had moved out with a family of his own and Jess, twenty-two, was travelling overseas. But even though my days were busier than ever, as a single parent, I missed Mike more than I could ever have imagined. There was a hole in my life, a deep ache, which seemed to get worse the longer he was away. Mike continued to be a wonderful father and foster father, and he was always around to help out when we needed him. But I slowly accepted that our marriage was over. We divorced in March 2013, a day filled with immeasurable sadness.

31

Some months later, I somehow allowed one of my friends to talk me into going on a blind date with a man named Pete, who she used to work with. I didn't want a new relationship. But as always, I gave in to the persuasion, without listening to my own feelings. I had been dreading the evening, but when it came around, I rather enjoyed putting on a nice dress, high heels and perfume. It felt years since I'd done anything for myself. I couldn't remember the last time I'd even worn lipstick. But the date itself, in a local pub, was filled with long silences and the evening dragged. Yet as I was buttoning my coat, I heard myself agreeing to see him again, even though I didn't want to.

As had always been my weakness, I seemed to be incapable of expressing my own wishes. Instead of doing what I wanted, I always ended up swept along as part of some else's plans. I didn't really know how to say no without hurting his feelings.

We met for a drink the following week, but, staring into my lemonade, again I found we'd hardly anything to say to each other. The evening passed excruciatingly slowly and I couldn't wait to hurry off home on my own. By the time Pete called me that weekend, I'd plucked up courage to tell him how I felt. 'This just isn't working,' I said. 'I'm so sorry.' We said goodbye a little awkwardly, but I felt relieved it was over.

'How did it go?' Jane texted.

'Two dates and it's over!' I replied. 'You know me, I'm happy on my own.'

The next day, I was surprised to wake up to a text from Pete. 'Shall we meet later?' I ignored it, but by that evening I had three more messages. By the end of the week, my phone was pinging several times a day. He just didn't seem to want to listen. When Hannah spotted the list of messages on my phone, she frowned.

'Mum, this isn't right,' she said. 'You hardly know this man. You should report him.'

'Oh, the police have more important things to worry about,' I replied, but even as I spoke, my phone pinged again. 'OK,' I agreed reluctantly.

I called the police that same evening, and explained I was being harassed by a man I had only just met. 'We only went on two dates,' I explained. 'But now, he won't leave me alone. Could you maybe have a word with him for me?'

32

The two police officers at my door looked professional and compassionate. One male, one female, they took their places on kitchen chairs while I perched nervously on the edge of a stool.

'I've made such a terrible mistake,' I told them. 'I went on a date with someone, even though I didn't want to. I only saw him twice but now he's texting me all the time and I don't know what to do.'

The female officer seemed very sympathetic, but it was her male colleague who took the main role, noting down everything I told him before taking copies of the text messages from Pete. I was glad that my previous dealings with the police, through my fostering work, had eased my nerves a little. I had reached the stage where I could hold a conversation with an officer without curling up inside.

'We'll be in touch,' he promised. 'But please let us know if he contacts you again in the meantime. We'll be having a word with him today.'

After they left, I felt much better. Surely this was the end of it.

The next morning, I hadn't been home long from dropping Hannah at school when the doorbell rang. I was surprised to see the male officer from the day before on my doorstep. He looked very smart and efficient in his uniform. He had dark hair and looked likely to be in his late thirties, only a little older than my son.

'PC Darren Heath,' he said. 'I'm sure you remember me. May I come in?'

'Yes, of course,' I said. 'Is there any news about Pete?'

'Not yet,' PC Heath replied. 'But I was passing and I just thought, I'll pop in to check on Kathy and have a coffee with her. One sugar please.'

As I switched on the kettle, I was impressed. I hadn't expected the police to be this attentive and take my complaint so seriously.

'So,' I asked, as I stirred in the milk. 'Have you spoken with him yet?'

'Oh, we've had words,' he said vaguely, and smiled.

I realised he probably couldn't keep me updated on the investigation for legal reasons.

I was just opening a packet of chocolate biscuits, when PC Heath said: 'So, Kathy, what do you do for fun? How do you spend your weekends?'

'Er, well, I don't really do much,' I said awkwardly, aware he was holding my gaze intently.

'You're very welcome to come out with me one night,' he said, and I couldn't help laughing.

'You're very funny,' I replied, 'but I don't think so. I think I'm past all that. I'll leave the partying to the young ones like you.'

He finished his coffee and left. But, two days later, he was back again.

'Get the kettle on,' he said with a charming smile. 'One sugar, remember?'

He did seem a little overfamiliar but then I thought this was probably his way of putting me at ease. The kettle hadn't even boiled when Jane turned up.

'Ah, so you're helping Kathy,' she said to PC Heath. 'I'm so glad.'

PC Heath nodded but he'd barely had a sip of his coffee when he stood up and announced he had to leave.

After the door closed, Jane said: 'There is something a bit weird about him. I think he's after you. I saw the way he was looking at you. He definitely fancies you.'

'No, don't be silly,' I replied. 'He was just calling round, making sure I'm OK. Neighbourhood policing. It's very kind of him.'

Jane shook her head. 'It's more than that. He's after you, I can tell.'

'Darren Heath is a police officer,' I spluttered. 'He's completely trustworthy. Beyond reproach. Anyway what can I do? I can't report him just because you think he's weird. He's here to help me, Jane. He's the police.'

A few days later, she called in to check I was OK. While we were chatting, I spotted PC Health walking up the path.

'Hello,' I said, as I opened the door. 'Is there any news?'

'Not yet,' he replied.

'Would you like a coffee?' I asked. 'I've just made one for my friend, Jane. You met her the other day.'

'Oh, in that case I won't stay,' he said, backing away hastily.

Closing the door, I had to admit I was a little surprised.

'He didn't want to come in because I was here,' Jane pointed out. 'He wanted you all to himself. You need to watch him, Kathy.'

I waved her concerns away. But that evening, my phone bleeped with a text message from PC Heath.

'It wasn't coffee I wanted when I called earlier,' said the message. 'It was your body.'

I felt sick inside. Was this his idea of a joke? I knew his behaviour was wrong, yet, as with the caretaker, as with my grandad, as with Fred West, there was no way I could speak out. I had only just scraped together enough confidence to have a conversation with a police officer. Complaining about him would be a different matter completely. Who would believe me, a lonely, divorced, middle-aged mum, over a respected serving police officer? It was ludicrous. And what would he see in me, anyway? I was old enough to be his mum. I convinced myself that he just had a strange sense of humour, a quirky personality. That I was being oversensitive. Overdramatic. Again.

The following week, PC Heath was back.

'Pete messaged me again earlier,' I said. 'Did you speak to him at all?'

'Oh,' he replied. 'The police work in strange ways. Anyway, what are you doing tonight, Kathy?'

Jane's warning rang out in my head, and I stuttered a little. 'Oh, er, nothing. But you're here to talk about Pete, aren't you?'

'OK,' he replied, without breaking eye contact. 'Well, let's see – did you and Pete sleep together?'

My jaw dropped. I almost had to stifle a laugh, I was so shocked. I couldn't believe what I'd heard.

'I have an appointment, actually,' I stammered, blushing deep red. 'I need to leave – sorry. Right away.'

I ran to the hallway to get my coat and showed him out. Watching him leave, through the side window, I was stunned to see him turn round and wink at me, as though we shared a racy secret. With clammy hands, I called Jane.

'You won't believe this!' I gasped. 'PC Heath called round and asked about my sex life. Then I just watched him wink at me as he left the house.'

'I told you!' Jane shrieked. 'He's weird! He's stalking you. Don't let him in again.'

All evening, I fretted. How had this happened? I blamed myself, worrying that perhaps I had led PC Heath on by making him coffee and offering him biscuits. I had meant to be friendly, nothing more, grateful that he was helping me. But perhaps I'd given out the wrong signals. Perhaps, as with Fred West, as with the abusers from my childhood, I was to blame. But I couldn't work out why PC Heath didn't seem interested in my harassment complaint at all. My temples thrummed with the warning signs of a seizure, and I tried to breathe slowly. It was a ridiculous, dangerous accusation, doubting a police officer like this. I was becoming paranoid. I was losing my grip. Yet I felt so alone and helpless. I'd made such a mess of my life. With the exception of Mike, every man I ever met, in whatever setting, seemed to turn on me.

This is what you deserve, Kathy. You're worth nothing. People are entitled to treat you however they fancy.

Added to the stress of the harassment, I had serious money troubles, too. And so, with a heavy heart, I decided to put our house on the market. The idea of losing our family home was devastating, but I could see no other way out. Besides, I couldn't stay here. I didn't feel safe any longer, with PC Heath calling round each day and making suggestive comments. The only solution was to move away somewhere new, somewhere nobody would find me. I was dreading asking Mike's permission – it was half his house, after all, and he had every right to be angry. But as I explained my plans down the phone, he was lovely, and as understanding and supportive as he had always been.

'You do what you have to do, Kathy,' he said. 'I'll sign the paperwork.'

Mike's compassion plucked at my heart strings, and I found myself blurting it all out: PC Heath's strange behaviour and my sadness over our divorce. These were my problems, not Mike's. Yet he was kindness itself, even offering to stay overnight at the house, in the spare room, to make sure I was safe. I felt so lucky to call him my friend, but I wanted to try and manage on my own. This mess was nothing to do with Mike, after all.

A few days later, the For Sale sign went up outside our family home and I was swamped with feelings of guilt and despair. This was all my fault. Again, I was running away – from a different monster this time, but I felt just as wretched as on all the other occasions. Sitting on the sofa, wiping away tears, my skin tightened when I spotted PC Heath walking up our path. This was the last thing I needed. I didn't want to let him in. Yet I couldn't bring myself to be rude to a police officer – it just wasn't in me.

'Why are you selling your house?' he asked, as soon as I answered the door.

'I'm short of money,' I said miserably. 'It's the only way.'

'It's not the only way!' he exclaimed. 'I'll sort it out for you.'

And then I watched, stunned, as he ran to the sign and began pulling it out of the ground.

'Please,' I begged in alarm. 'Please stop. Calm down and I'll make you a coffee.'

Bizarrely, I felt as though I was the one looking after him. I was annoyed at myself, believing I'd caused the whole incident by telling him about my money troubles.

'Please leave it,' I pleaded.

But he wouldn't listen. In the end, I left him in the garden, pulling at the sign, and I closed the door. I slid down the back of it until I slumped onto the carpet and my head fell into my hands.

You're in another awful mess, Kathy, I said to myself. *And it's all your own doing.*

33

The following Friday evening, Hannah was out helping at a local church group and so I was home alone. PC Heath knocked at the door and, without even waiting for me to say hello, he strode past me uninvited, through the kitchen and into the living room. He had never been in our living room before and my stomach lurched a little as I followed him. He sat on one of the two leather sofas, leaning back with his arms out as though he was sunbathing. Warily, I sat down on the other.

'Do you have news about the case?' I asked. 'Because I am still getting text messages. It's made no difference at all since I reported him. It's really stressing me out.'

Instead of replying, PC Heath stood up and came to sit on my sofa. He slid along the cushions until he was right next to me, his body sandwiched against mine. My heart pounding, I inched away from him, anxious not to seem rude, but desperate to get away. Yet each time I moved, he did too, until I was right at the end of the sofa, with the armrest barring my way.

So I stood up, walked to the other side of the room and asked again. 'So do you have news? What's happening with my complaint?'

'I've sorted him out,' PC Heath replied, leaning forward on the sofa as though trying to get nearer to me. 'That's all you need to know.'

He was staring intensely, and I felt a shiver run through me.

'But what does that mean?' I asked nervously, trying to fill the awkward silence.

PC Heath didn't appear to hear me. Instead, he grinned and said: 'So what do you reckon, Kathy? Do you fancy a bit with me?'

My mouth ran dry and my stomach pitched and rolled as though I was about to be sick. Or, worse, suffer a seizure. I was instantly and painfully aware that I was all alone in a house with a man who was much fitter and stronger than I was. Who wanted me to have sex with him. I thought immediately of Fred West, of the caretaker, of my grandad. Did PC Heath know about them and think he could abuse me too? Was I a sitting duck, an easy target? Was that the real reason he was here? I even doubted, in my panic, that he was a genuine police officer. Perhaps this whole thing had been a charade, right from the start. Like Fred West and his fake happy family. Like the smoke rings my father used to blow – enticing and mysterious, but never what they seemed. Dragging my thoughts back to reality, I forced myself to look at PC Heath, to try not to look as frightened as I felt. I had to find a way out of this. Like all of my abusers from the past, he was smiling, leering at me, as though there was something vaguely amusing about the whole situation. It was bizarre that I seemed to attract predators in this way, and that none of them took me seriously. It was a joke, a bit of light-hearted entertainment for them all. What was wrong with me? But as PC Heath leaned further towards me, his eyes suddenly as cold as chips of ice, I felt a stab of terror. This was no joke. I was in real danger now.

As a roar of panic sounded in my ears, the doorbell suddenly rang, loud and triumphant. In that moment, so many images flashed through my mind, reminders of all the times I had been saved:

The ferry to England, leaving my childhood abusers behind

Shirley, walking out of the living room and ordering Fred to put me down

Deirdre, rushing into the bedroom when Fred was on top of me

The unknown man, shouting Fred's name when he was in my bed

The unknown caller ringing the doorbell when Fred and Rose had me trapped

And now, my own doorbell.

Choking back tears of relief, I ran to open it.

'Hey, Mum, are you OK?' Jess asked. 'You look white as a sheet. I'm not coming in, I'm just dropping off some books for—'

'No,' I insisted, with a hard stare. 'You must come in. Really. You must.'

Jess looked at me strangely but allowed me to drag her into the living room.

'Pleased to meet you,' she said, shaking PC Heath's hand. 'Are you here about Pete? Have you spoken to him?'

'No,' PC Heath replied.

'Why not?' Jess asked, in her typically straightforward way.

'Well,' he said, pulling his mouth into a thin line. 'That's not how things work.'

Jess stared at him. 'I think it is,' she said firmly.

PC Heath was already hurrying out of the door as she spoke.

I didn't want to worry her, but after he'd gone, I confessed I was feeling a little out of my depth.

'He's not doing anything to help,' I said. 'He just comes round for coffee every day. He's not interested.'

'Mum, you must ring the police immediately,' Jess said. 'Tell them what you told me. There is something wrong.'

'He *is* the police,' I replied wearily. 'I haven't the energy to make a complaint, not with everything else that's going on. And nobody would believe me anyway.'

But I knew she was right. And the next time PC Heath called round, I checked the peephole before putting on my coat and grabbing my door keys.

'Sorry, I'm just on my way out,' I called, opening the open living-room window a notch. 'I can't let you in today. Family emergency.'

Another time, I pretended to be out and hid upstairs in the bathroom until he left. I was terrified of going downstairs, in case he spotted me through the front window and banged on the door. It was like being back at Cromwell Street, trapped in my own home, unable even to blink without feeling someone was watching me. I had always felt safe and happy in my lovely home, but now I felt hemmed in and suffocated. I was careful not to stand in the window, or to go in the garden, or to leave the house without checking the street first. PC Heath continued to knock on the door while I hid behind the sofa. Calling the police had made the situation so much worse. Now I had two problems instead of one.

'This could only happen to me,' I joked, when Jane called round.

But I was struggling to cope. The pressure grew worse and

worse, until I felt as though my lungs were solidifying and I was snatching at pockets of oxygen. I could hardly breathe. Though I was cooking daily for Hannah, I could not face food myself. And I barely slept. In my nightmares, I saw Shirley, reaching for me, her fingertips brushing mine, agonisingly close, until she fell away, pixelating into blackness. Other nights, I dreamed Fred was looming over me, his doughy face pressed against mine, his demonic giggle ringing in my ears. Even in my sleep, I could smell him, that foul stench which I now knew was the dried blood of human remains. When I woke, cold with fear, I was not sure how much more I could take.

Six weeks after I had first reported Pete to the police, three officers knocked on my door. There were two men and one woman, all wearing plain clothes and grim expressions.

'We believe you've been dealing with Darren Heath,' said the female officer. 'We've had a complaint about him. We'd like to come in please.'

I had a sudden rush of paranoia. What if these people were working with PC Heath? What if they were here to entrap me? Did they know about the caretaker and about my grandad? Did they know I'd been assaulted by Fred West? Perhaps they were here to attack me, too. Maybe they were here to arrest me for not reporting the abuse? It was ridiculous but, as my mind raced along like a rollercoaster, I no longer knew who to trust. I had been failed and let down so many times, lurching from one agony to the next, that I was losing my grip on reality.

'Can the two men please wait in the car?' I asked timidly. 'I'll speak to the female officer on her own, if that's OK.'

It was the first time I could remember ever standing up for

myself, and it took a lot of courage, especially against someone in authority. But it was a matter of self-preservation and the two men agreed to wait outside.

In the kitchen, the female officer said to me: 'We suspect that Heath has been targeting women for many years. Can I ask if his behaviour towards you has been in any way unprofessional or inappropriate?'

'Yes,' I admitted. 'It has. I've been so worried about it, but I was too scared to say anything.'

The officer explained that the husband of one of the women Heath had been targeting had made a complaint and he was now under investigation, accused of having sex with vulnerable women he was supposed to protect. My hand flew to my mouth as she spoke.

'He asked me to have sex with him,' I told her. 'I didn't know what to do, with him being a police officer. But then my daughter called round. She saved me from him, I'm sure of it. Another time, he sent me a racy text message. And he asked me about my sex life. My friend said he was weird but I just thought he was being friendly.'

It took over an hour to give my statement and by the end of it I was in tears.

'Why am I a magnet for predators?' I wept. 'Why me? Do I have a tattoo on my forehead or a sign on my door?'

The police officer shook her head sadly. 'Please don't think like that,' she said. 'This is not your fault, and his behaviour has nothing to do with you.'

If I was brutally honest, I was not especially surprised by the revelations. This was no more than I deserved. Heath was simply a link in the long chain of abuse. And as I dried my eyes,

I realised I had, once again, been incredibly lucky, too. In this instance, as with those before it, I had escaped by the skin of my teeth. Every time I had been targeted, it could have been so much worse.

Before she left, the officer explained that Heath had been arrested but was out on bail. She gave me an emergency number to call in case he turned up again.

'Please call me day or night if you see him,' she said.

Later that day, officers came to fit cameras inside and outside my home. The cameras gave me some security but I was still panic-stricken, unable to relax, as I scanned the street. That week, one of my friends came to cut my hair and I made a joke about the cameras.

'You had better make a good job of my trim, because we're both being filmed,' I laughed, pointing to the lens. 'You might get arrested for giving me a dodgy hairdo.'

This was something I had always done – made light of trauma, refused to acknowledge the most serious situations. But at my core I was crumbling, like an eroding cliff. Chunk after chunk of me was falling into the sea and soon there would be nothing left at all.

My friend hadn't been gone long when I heard a noise outside. I went to the window, thinking perhaps she'd left something behind. But my blood froze when I spotted Heath at my garden gate.

'No!' I gasped.

With trembling fingers, I managed to dial the emergency number. Crouching behind the sofa, I was too afraid even to get up and lock the doors in case Heath spotted me.

It felt like hours, but within a couple of minutes I heard the screech of sirens outside. Still, despite the commotion, I didn't dare look out. It was only afterwards, when there was a knock at the door, that I felt strong enough to peer through the peephole. Standing on my doorstep was the female officer who had taken my statement.

'Kathleen, we just want to let you know that Heath has been removed,' she said. 'You're safe. Thank you for calling us.'

Staggering back into the living room, I was suddenly aware of a strong smell of tar. It was so intense, I was convinced there must be workmen laying a driveway somewhere nearby. But then I began to feel sickly and dizzy. The smell of tar grew stronger and, mixed in, to my disgust, was the unmistakable stench of Fred West, that rotten smell of decay. Human decay. Panicked that I was about to vomit, I got up to run to the bathroom but made it only as far as the rug in front of the fire. As I felt my legs give way, I managed to dial Mike's number.

'Help,' I mumbled, my voice muffled in the rug. 'Help me, Mike.'

When I came round, I was in hospital, linked up to machines. Mike was at my bedside, his kind face creased with worry.

I found you collapsed on the living-room floor,' he explained. 'You've had a massive seizure. You were completely out of it.'

I smiled weakly. Even in my semi-conscious blur, I was aware that, yet again, I had dodged another disaster.

'You saved me,' I said. 'Thank you.'

I managed to sit up and sip some water, and I explained to Mike how Heath had turned up outside the house and the stress had triggered the seizure.

'Look, let's accept the first offer we get for the house,' Mike said. 'We need to sell it so you can move away somewhere new where they won't find you.'

'But it's our family home,' I whispered.

Mike shook his head and smiled. 'Home is wherever you make it,' he said. 'Nothing is worth this stress. Let's get the sale through as quickly as we can.'

Seeing his eyes filled with care and concern, I felt a sudden rush of longing. The words landed in my mouth from nowhere and, like pebbles, I rolled them around my tongue until they were smooth and shiny. But could I ever find the courage to say them out loud? Perhaps I was clouded by the after-effects of the seizure, because for the first time in my life, I heard myself saying exactly what I thought, without a single worry for the consequences.

'I have missed you so much, Mike, I really have. I still love you and I always will.'

'Me too,' Mike said, reaching across my pillow to kiss me. 'I love you, Kathy.'

At peace with the world, I closed my eyes and smiled. Despite the stress, the abuse, the stalking and the seizures, I was flooded with happiness. For there, among the burning wreckage of my life, was a small seedling of hope. I had lost everything, and yet I had everything I needed.

34

Our family home sold quickly and while it was a great wrench it was also, strangely, a relief. I had to get away from the place. Though I hadn't seen Heath since the day of my seizure, the memory lingered on, like a shadow across my consciousness. Packing up the last of our belongings, I acknowledged I was running away again. But I had no choice. Mike was renting a flat at Gloucester Docks and it turned out the unit next to his was empty.

'I'll take it,' I said. 'For Hannah and me.'

It was only temporary, and it felt nice, having Mike so close by. I felt safe again. We bumped into each other most mornings and afternoons. And in the evenings, I invited him round and cooked for us all together.

'This is ridiculous,' he said eventually. 'There is no point in us paying two lots of rent and two lots of bills. Let's all move in together.'

'That is a great idea,' I agreed.

Hannah and I moved in with him that same afternoon. It was cramped but happy and it would be several years before a council property became available for us. Our new home, when we eventually found it, was lovely – away from the city centre, with fields nearby and a church next door. It was peaceful there and I hoped we had found somewhere we could stay for good.

The case against Heath moved quickly and it was a relief to hear he had pleaded guilty so I was not required to give evidence in court. Even so, the police asked if I would appear, along with the other victims, at sentence, to have our impact statements heard. Though it was upsetting to have to go to the Crown Court, especially after the Rose West trial, I was anxious to see justice done. And curious, too, to meet the other women he had targeted.

On the morning of the sentencing, in March 2015, I was collected by an officer and taken to the police headquarters. In the police canteen, over cups of tea, I exchanged stories with the other victims. Some women had been through true horror at his hands and, once more, I felt as though I had got away at the last moment. I had outrun the monster again. Like me, they had trusted him, unable to believe or accept that a police officer would behave so abhorrently. He had hidden behind his uniform. Fred West had hidden behind his DIY skills. Was anything as it seemed? I remembered my father's smoke rings, and I felt my spirits sag.

At Bristol Crown Court, that afternoon, Darren Heath, forty-five, was sentenced to three years and nine months in prison. He had previously admitted five charges of misconduct in a public office by engaging in sexual relationships with three women he had met while on duty between July 2002 and December 2013.

Heath, a former police constable with Gloucestershire Police, also admitted misconduct by exposing himself to one of his victims between September 2012 and February 2013. He pleaded guilty to continually attending the home of a woman under the guise of investigating an allegation that someone was harassing her. That woman was me. To my astonishment, the judge said Heath had been planning on having a relationship with me. It was madness, utter madness. For the thousandth time in my life, I asked myself why on earth I seemed to attract such trouble.

In sentencing, Neil Ford QC described Heath's behaviour as 'corrosive to the reputation of the police service generally'. Heath was described as 'manipulative and calculating' by the Gloucestershire police force. But for all the damage he had caused, the sentencing seemed very light to me. Afterwards a TV reporter requested to speak with one of the victims about the case and I volunteered. But I was in something of a daze as he asked me a few questions in a small room in the court building.

When I got home, I tried to erase the court hearing and the interview from my mind. But memories of Heath's behaviour ricocheted around my head, and I could not get rid of them. My faith in the police had been completely shattered. I had held them in such high regard, yet they had fallen so far. I could not, even in an emergency, have called on them. Darren Heath had single-handedly destroyed the fragile trust it had taken me so long to build. For me, that was as serious as the harassment itself.

In 2020, almost five years on from the case, I started a new job in a care home. One evening, with the residents all bathed and tucked up in bed, I was making my way down the corridor when I heard my own voice coming out of the staffroom. Perplexed,

I hurried in and found that one of my colleagues was playing a recording of my voice out of her phone.

'Is this you, Kathy?' she asked. 'I had no idea you were a victim of that pervert policeman. But this is definitely you, isn't it?'

I stared at her in disbelief as I unravelled her words. I couldn't work out how she knew about Heath, or how my voice was coming out of her phone. She showed me a link to the interview I'd given years earlier. The video showed my hands and my jacket. And my voice, on the audio, was clearly identifiable. Gasping, I handed her the phone back. I'd had no idea the interview was being filmed, or that it had been posted online and had presumably been available for the past five years. I was mortified. With all the fuss, several colleagues gathered round, each one dumbfounded as they recognised my voice.

'Kathy, we didn't realise you had been stalked,' they said. 'How awful. What a rotten copper he was. You must have been devastated.'

'I'm just nipping outside,' I mumbled.

Gulping in fresh air, as the tears rolled down my cheeks, I was once again overcome with those old feelings of shame and guilt. It was my fault Heath had targeted me, my fault I was now on the Internet and my fault I had been named and shamed in front of all my new workmates. I gave my notice in the next day and left the job as soon as I could.

For months and years afterwards, I dreaded anyone finding the clip online, most of all my own children and family. I felt I was the one exposed, not Heath. I didn't think I had any right to have it removed. People like me didn't matter, and the TV reporter had confirmed that for me.

*

Into 2021, life settled into a steady rhythm, with Mike working as a driver, Hannah doing well at college and me enjoying a new job as a project leader in the care system. John was settled with his own family and Jess was still travelling; now working around Asia. Though I missed her terribly, it was a comfort to know she was fulfilling her dreams.

One warm, balmy evening in May 2021, Mike and I were eating a chicken salad, swapping anecdotes from work, while the TV hummed in the background. I paid it no attention, until the news headlines came on.

'Police are set to excavate a cafe in Gloucester in the search for a suspected victim of serial killer Fred West.'

With a clatter, I let my cutlery fall onto my plate. 'No!' I choked. 'Not again!'

Mike reached for my hand as the newsreader announced how a teenager named Mary Bastholm, who had worked at the cafe close to Cromwell Street, had gone missing in January 1968. Mary, fifteen, had disappeared on her way to catch a bus to visit her boyfriend and had not been seen since. The newsreader revealed Fred West had actually confessed to a family member that he had murdered Mary. He was thought to have carried out renovation work in the toilets and the cellar at the cafe in 1968 and was known to be a regular at the cafe, now called the Clean Plate but formerly known as the Pop-In.

'The Pop-In!' I gasped. 'I don't believe it.'

Deirdre had bought me breakfast at the Pop-In cafe to celebrate my eighteenth birthday, so many years ago. In more recent times, Jane and I had often met at the Pop-In for a cup of tea and a chat. We loved it there. It was a horrible coincidence, nothing more, yet I felt somehow linked with Mary, as I was with the other victims – our secrets irreversibly knotted together. Once again, I had to face the possibility that one of Fred's victims had been buried under my feet, that she had lain hidden as I ordered toasted teacakes and chatted. The horror was following me around.

'Why can't they just leave this alone?' I muttered. 'People are trying to get on with their lives, and this rakes it all back up again.'

It was like ripping off a scab and making it bleed all over again. There could be no healing if we were constantly haunted by our pasts. And yet, even as I spoke, I thought of the poor girl's family, and how they had waited over fifty years to find out where she was. Did the excavation risk raising their hopes in vain and prolonging their agony, or could it be the closure they needed? I was torn. Mary's photo was shown on television. She looked so young, with big, innocent eyes, and I felt my heart crack and break a little. I remembered Fred's wandering hands, his foul breath, his manic laughter. I hoped, above all else, she had not met her end through him. The news report explained that the cafe was now, ironically, owned by a charity that supported women who were victims of violence. It was yet another twist of fate, another coil in the tangled story of Cromwell Street.

'Are you OK, love?' Mike asked. 'Try and finish your salad.'

But my stomach was clenched tight. I knew there was no way I could swallow a single morsel. Playing in my mind was a slideshow of evil, fragments of memory, glued together by fear: Fred and Rose dragging me off the pavement, Fred pinning me to the sofa while Rose stroked my hair, Fred climbing into my bed and assaulting me as I slept . . .

'I can smell Fred West,' I said in confusion. 'He smells like tar.'

The stench filled my nostrils and expanded, like foam, inside my skull. Realising I was going to vomit, I stumbled into the downstairs bathroom. Lifting the lid of the toilet, I knelt down, preparing to be sick. But then, everything went blank. When I came round, I was in hospital, with Hannah at my bedside.

'You had a massive seizure, Mam,' she told me. 'Do you remember?'

I shook my head groggily. There were snippets of recollection: waiting in A&E, bickering with Hannah because I was hungry, insisting I wanted to go home. But, mostly, I didn't remember a thing. The doctors decided to admit me for tests and, after a brain scan, I was formally diagnosed with epilepsy. After nearly six decades of seizures, my condition finally had a name. I was prescribed medication and told I would lose my driving licence. It was a blow, but I understood it was for my own safety. X-rays later showed I had damaged my shoulder and broken my foot when I fell.

'I'm sorry, Mrs Richards, this is all such bad news,' a doctor said.

I nodded vaguely but my thoughts were elsewhere. Even in hospital, I was hooked on the news reports about the search for Mary Bastholm. The police said they had received reports from a TV crew of some blue material found buried at the cafe. Mary was known to have been wearing a blue coat and carrying a blue bag when she disappeared. My stomach lurched at the connection. Officers had been brought in and were searching six 'voids' around half a metre beneath the toilet floor. A specialist team of archaeologists and anthropologists were working painstakingly on each void in turn. Two days on, I was allowed home from hospital to recuperate at home. I couldn't get around because of my broken foot, and I was bruised and shaken from my fall. My medication was also quite powerful, and it would take some time for me to adapt. Stuck in the living room, with my foot up on the sofa, I found myself immersed, once again, in the trauma of Cromwell Street. The cafe excavation brought it all back in painful technicolour. I thought a lot about Shirley and her baby. Had poor Mary suffered as Shirley had? I didn't even know what had happened to Shirley's remains or where she had been laid to rest. I didn't know who to ask. There was no end to it, and the ghosts floated around me. They were with me, always.

In one news report, the senior investigating officer, DCI John Turner, revealed he had spoken with Fred West's son. Fred had apparently told his son he had murdered Mary years earlier. DCI Turner said: 'Fred lied to a lot of people, sent police off on wild goose chases all around the country, which has been heartbreaking over the years for lots of family members including the Bastholms. Just because Fred said he did it, it doesn't mean to say he did. Fred most definitely played with investigators, he wanted to control the investigation, he enjoyed being the centre of attention and he was toying with us at times.'

The words rang cold and true in my ears. It seemed Fred had played the police just as he had played me. Absolutely, he had enjoyed the spotlight and revelled in the control. He had toyed with me, too, pinning me against the wall, squeezing me and pressing me. Even under suspicion of murder, even when dealing with the police, it seemed Fred's character had not changed one bit. *Always the clown.* Two weeks after the investigation had started, it was announced that no human remains had been found. The excavation finished at the end of May and Mary's family said, in a distressing statement:

> We were hoping to get a final closure on her disappearance so that we could put her to rest. We have been open-minded throughout this process and we now know that the cafe can be ruled out. Mary was a strong-willed and happy-go-lucky teenager dearly loved by her parents and two brothers. She enjoyed life and was just coming into her own when her life was tragically cut short.

35

The excavations at the cafe had prompted another period of personal soul-searching, as once again I was tormented with an onslaught of reminders of my trauma at Cromwell Street. No matter what anyone told me, I was convinced I was responsible for Shirley's death. The guilt solidified and cemented over time, and I was dragged down low by it. I couldn't work because of my epilepsy and, for the first time in many years, I had time on my hands. But I didn't know what to do with it. My solace, stuck at home all day, was to clean. Even now, hoovering and polishing brightened my soul in a way I couldn't really explain. If only my inner turmoil was so easy to sweep away. Instead, a necrotising force, it ate away at me from the inside.

I was heartbroken for my eight-year-old self, broken into pieces for a paltry penny by a dirty old paedophile who did not even have to threaten me to get his way. Perversely, I wished he had been violent towards me. Perhaps then I wouldn't have held myself responsible for so many years. And with each incident of abuse, what little self-esteem I'd had was eroded further and further. By the time I met Fred West, I felt I had no option but to suffer his appalling abuse in silence. Into adulthood, I was gripped by a belief that I simply was not good enough. I could not speak directly to doctors, priests or teachers. I never stayed at a hotel or ate at a fancy restaurant. I didn't buy nice clothes. I always felt those luxuries were reserved for others, not for me. I was not on that level and not of that calibre. And there, the real, pernicious damage of the sexual abuse was laid bare. It's not the assaults themselves, though they were horrific. It's the long-lasting harm, the self-loathing, the worthlessness, which creeps like mould into the darkest corners of the soul. I had spent a lifetime fighting the belief that I was worth only a single penny. And no more. That horrible man took my innocence, my happiness and my self-belief. He paid me very little. Yet the cost to me was so great, I was still paying for it five decades later. And I was at breaking point. Something had to give.

The police had offered me counselling, following the Darren Heath trial, and I decided I was finally ready to speak to someone about it. Or, at least, I felt so desperate I was willing to give it a try.

In the first session, my misgivings rushed out in a torrent, as I described how I had let Shirley down.

The counsellor frowned. 'I don't understand what you mean. How is it your fault? You had no part in her death at all.'

I sighed. She didn't understand. Nobody did.

Week after week, I returned to see the counsellor. I spoke only about Shirley – how I could, *should*, have saved her life. How I felt complicit in everything that went wrong.

'You have PTSD from a survivor's guilt,' the counsellor said gently. 'That isn't the same as being responsible or in any way implicated in her death. None of this was your fault.'

Though I tried, I still could not bring myself to confide in her about my own abuse. She knew nothing of what I had been through as a child and nothing of the way Fred and Rose had targeted me. Really, I did not see it as significant; I did not see that I mattered. And part of me was still afraid she might call the police and I'd be arrested for not reporting Fred back in 1978. I had brainwashed myself so effectively that I believed I might be criminally responsible. My secrets rotted away inside me, spreading a poison that I feared might one day be the end of me.

It should have been you, Kathy.

But as the months passed, I started to feel some slow-burning benefit from the therapy. Gradually, I realised that my arguments against myself were illogical and deeply unfair. How could I, a child, have tackled two dangerous serial killers on my own? And I didn't even know they *were* killers. I couldn't have spoken to the police about my own abuse because I was traumatised and so used to being abused that I thought I didn't count. The overt messages to me, from my parents, from my abusers, were that I did not matter. And I had taken that mantra to heart. For many years, I had listened helplessly to those who wanted to destroy me.

Yet there were other voices too, precious diamonds in those gloomy years: Diane inviting me to her wedding; my friend Sally and her dolls; the kind nurse at the hospital after my overdose. I had a wonderful husband and my beloved children. I had good friends, like Jane. All of these elements outshone the evil. I was beginning to see that now and I realised I should have focused on their voices instead. This was not a sudden or immediate conversion, but more of a slow awakening, a new petal opening each day. I had always enjoyed reading, and I started to read self-help books alongside my therapy. On each page, I found little nuggets of advice and support, which I hugged close to me.

Finally, wonderfully, I understood and accepted that I was not to blame for any of the abuse. Not one moment of it. I was not responsible for the caretaker stealing away my innocence as a small child. Neither was I to blame when my grandad groomed and abused me. I was not in any way at fault for any of the abuse from Fred and Rose West. And – perhaps this was hardest of all to grasp – I was not to blame for Shirley's murder, or for any of the other murders. I was a victim, not a perpetrator. Yes, I was lucky to have survived, I was fortunate to be alive and I had a duty to enjoy my life to the full and make the most of my second chance. With acceptance came freedom; I felt lighter and brighter. Taking deep breaths, I found I could fill my lungs for the first time since I was eight years old. I was not the worthless, pointless, hopeless individual I had painted myself as. I realised I deserved fancy hotels, birthday gifts and new dresses after all. I deserved affection, friendship and love. And not because of the abuse, or even despite the abuse. But just because I am the same as everyone else and we all deserve to be treated with respect. I had always viewed happiness as a nebulous and distant concept, meant for others but not for me. Now I saw I had been wrong – and wronged. And it was time for positive change. Against all my instincts, late in 2023, I booked a fancy hotel in Tenerife for Mike and me.

'You deserve it,' I told myself, over and over, as I sat in the plush lounge and sipped my lemonade and lime. 'You've every right to be here, Kathy.'

And so, painstakingly, like a ship changing course, I began to look to the future. I lifted my head and, finally, I allowed myself to feel the sunshine on my face.

Mike and I had been back together for six years when, one Saturday morning, Hannah said to me, 'Don't you think it's about time you and Dad got married again?'

'What?' I gulped, as I buttered my morning toast. 'This is the first I've heard of it!'

'Well, you never really split up, did you?' she said, with the sort of straight talking a parent only ever hears from their child. 'The whole thing was ridiculous. You should get married again.'

Later, Mike and I laughed about her candour but we both agreed she was right. We were meant for each other. And it didn't feel right to me, not being Mrs Richards any more. We planned a small ceremony at Stroud Register Office in March 2022 for just ten people. I wore pale pink, Mike had his best suit on and Hannah, of course, was our guest of honour. Afterwards, we had a quiet meal with family. It was nothing like our first wedding, with the TV cameras and all the show and excitement. But to me, it was just as special. Mike was the only man I'd ever met whom I could love and trust, and I knew without doubt that I could count on him, no matter what.

Deirdre wasn't at our wedding and I got the news soon afterwards that she was very unwell. She had suffered a seizure and was being treated in hospital. Hannah and I drove over to Derby to visit her and I was shocked by her appearance in the hospital bed. She'd lost a lot of weight and she looked so fragile. In February 2024, she passed away, aged sixty-five. I was heartbroken. She and I had been through so much together. We had been best friends as children hunting for pennies, sweets and clean clothes, we had kept each other afloat through our teenage years and supported each other at Cromwell Street. I had never spoken to her again about Fred West, yet I always felt the scars remained, deep inside her, as they did in me. It had hurt her terribly to see me suffer there. In some small way I believe the trauma contributed to her early passing. I imagine there are many other women whose lives have also been cut short like that. The thought makes me realise again how lucky I am.

Into 2025, Mike and I are living happily in retirement. I still enjoy cleaning, but then I have always found cleaning more relaxing than relaxing! Even now, there is nothing I love more than a good declutter to clear my head. Hannah has started her own cleaning business, she's a chip off the old block. She's still living at home and it's lovely to have her close by. She and I are best pals. We have two rescue dogs – Maggie, who is eighteen months old and looks like a spaniel-corgi cross, and Nellie, who is aged six and looks a little like a pug. My dogs are great therapy, and we enjoy long walks daily. My love of animals stems back to our beloved German shepherd, Duke, and our horse, Jacko. I often wonder, still, what became of them, what became of Polly my doll, what became of all that I loved and lost. Yet now, without regret, I can look back with affection and nostalgia.

My epilepsy is under control and I haven't had any seizures for the last couple of years. It doesn't seems coincidental that they cleared up when my stress improved. I am more inclined to believe I have psychogenic nonepileptic seizures (PNES), where seizures are related to psychological distress and trauma rather than to abnormal electrical activity in the brain. I feel my seizures are closely linked to the abuse. As my confidence has increased, my stutter has faded and I rarely stammer now. Like so many bad memories, it is consigned to the past, to what now feels like another life. Now I can look back on my phone-box misery and giggle at my teenage self. Laughter in the dark – like cleaning – has got me through the worst of times.

My three children are doing well and I'm so proud of them all. I'm still in touch with many of our foster children, too, who bring their own children to see me. They call me 'Nanny Kath'. Being a mother, both to my own kids and to others, has been the greatest gift of my life. The termination is never far from my thoughts. My children are not replacements for the baby I could have had but, over time, they have helped me heal from the debilitating pain left behind. Have I forgiven myself completely? No. But I am trying.

I live in the countryside, seventeen miles from Gloucester, and I avoid passing Cromwell Street at all costs, even though there is nothing there now except an expanse of concrete and some greenery down the side of the walkway. Much as I don't want to go near the place, I won't let the past drive me from my home and I'm happy here in rural Gloucestershire. Incredibly, thirty years since the trial, visitors continue to flock to the site. Recent reports claim there are thousands of visitors every year and there are even official tours around Gloucester. This sort of thing is known, apparently, as dark tourism. I can understand how people unconnected to the West family might have a fascination with what happened, along with a desire to understand it, so it can be prevented from happening again. But those, like me, who are closest to the tragedy are the ones who seem to stay furthest away.

In February this year, my mother passed away, aged ninety-one, following a burst aneurysm in her stomach. I went to see her in the Chapel of Rest and I had a long chat with her.

'Thank you for being the best Mam you could,' I told her. 'And thank you for saving my life at Cromwell Street. I'll never ever forget that. I owe you one, Mam.'

Before I left, I bought a necklace with her fingerprint inside it, and I've worn it ever since. Thanks to the necklace, I feel like my mother is close to me, something I longed for all the years she was alive.

Writing this book has made me realise just how lucky I have been in my life. Time and time again, I have escaped the monsters breathing down my neck. I feel certain I must have a little angel sitting on my shoulder and keeping me safe. My heartache all started with that first strawberry sweet and my childhood was dominated by abuse, poverty and hunger. Then, as an adult, I was consumed with feelings of shame and guilt. I accepted long ago that I cannot change any of that. But I recognise now that I can change the ending. And that's why I wrote this book. I want other survivors to understand that you are never, ever to blame, so please, speak out and hold your heads high. With every word, every paragraph, every secret I have shared for the first time, Fred West's power over me has been dampened and doused until it has finally been extinguished. My book has been a cleansing experience, a catharsis, a little like a good clean-out for my mind. For over forty years, Fred West sat in my head, like a devil. Now he is gone for good and, at last, I can stop running.

271

Acknowledgements

To my amazing husband, Mike. You have been with me since the day we met over the garden fence. Your strength and support are truly remarkable. Thank you Mike xx.

To my three children, my happiest times were the days each of you were born. I am grateful to have you in my life xx.

To my dearest friend, Jane, thank you for being a part of my story.